God's timetable for the end of time!

by Oral Roberts

Contents

1

Our frustrated society

IN PRESIDENT RICHARD M. NIXON's inaugural address of January 20, 1969, he appraised our nation's weaknesses with candor, saying,

We have found ourselves rich in goods, but ragged in spirit; reaching with magnificent precision for the moon, but falling into raucous discord here on earth. We are caught in war, wanting peace. We are torn by division, wanting unity. We see around us empty lives, wanting fulfillment. We see tasks that need doing, waiting for hands to do them. To a crisis of the spirit, we need an answer of the spirit.

The perceptive Christian recognizes the fact that each successive crisis our burdened world faces is basically a spiritual one. And time is running out. God's timetable points to the midnight hour of human history minus very few minutes. Scientists and political thinkers have discerned this ominous threat and fear the worst.

We are living in troubled, crucial times and as we approach the last quarter of the 20th century we are confronted with awesome probabilities. Many hold little hope for Planet Earth's celebration of the year 2000. Enigmatic Communist China, with more than a fourth of the world's inhabitants and soon to be the possessor of the intercontinental ballistic missile, looms as a disturbing nuclear shadow even to the neighboring

5

Kremlin bureaucrats, as evidenced by the Sino-Soviet border clashes.

At the close of 1968 the General Assembly of the United Nations had an agenda so burdened with the problems of humanity that the crises conference calendar was full for three years. The new United Nations Demographic Book indicated an increase of 180,000 people each day in world growth. More than 3½ billion human beings will be inhabiting the world during the decade of the 70's, depending upon the wisdom of their leaders to solve the increasingly complex and demanding problems forced upon each nation. A physician who helped to develop the birth-control pill fears that the developing nations of the Far East are headed for the certain agony of famine in the 1970's. The population explosion, constant war tensions, recurring international monetary crises, violence on the streets and campuses throughout the world — these and many other perplexing issues cannot be avoided.

You cannot easily describe what is actually taking place. Some things you can only feel. I feel the icy breath of godlessness as immorality sweeps across the nations and it causes me to shudder in my spirit. And as I return to my beloved America after ministering abroad, I am increasingly disturbed by our own problems and pains which are screaming out for adequate and just solutions. Our Trojan horse of godlessness, divisiveness, and immorality seems to be a greater threat to our national solidarity and survival than the infiltration of Communism.

We are living in a society bent upon dissipating its greatness and hastening its self-destruction. Violence is common in many communities and upon an increas-

ing number of college campuses. Many youthful ideal-
ists have allied themselves with extremists who pro-
mote violence in order to dramatize problems such as
hard-core unemployment, racial discrimination, and in-
ferior education in ghetto schools. Martin Luther
King, Jr., to many the symbol of peaceful Gandhian
resistance, was cut down by an assassin's bullet. This
terminated the patience of many citizens who then
became susceptible to the hatred preached by the
revolutionaries.

Universities across the United States have experienced previously unheard-of harassments. Instead of
peaceful demonstrations and student strikes conducted
in an orderly manner, we now experience the barri-
caded administrative offices, the sacking of presidents'
offices, and the wanton destruction of campus property.
General student frustrations at being shortchanged in
their education and their ignored resentments have
supplied additional fuel to the incendiary activists who
comprise but a minute fraction of the college population.

Consider the distressing dope traffic. How many
permissive or inconsistent parents have attempted too
late to curb the harmful adventures of their children?
Smoking pot (marijuana) has become the in-thing,
spreading to the campus, high school, and even junior
high. Attempts to legalize its usage are being made
by those who believe that marijuana has no harmful
effects. However, psychological addiction fastens itself
upon its users, leaving them vulnerable targets for the
pushers of heroin and LSD.

Besides the supposed mind-expanding drugs that
are plaguing students, pornography is glutting the

7

lucrative youth market. Films, photographs, paper-backs and magazines display acts of homosexuality, Lesbianism, and sadistic violence. The love of money is the root of this evil, motivating the producers and peddlers of obscenity and smut. A film designed to show the evils of smut was shown recently to a group of Citizens for Youth Protection in Minneapolis. Seasoned case workers were shocked by "Target Smut" and decided that the film was unfit for public viewing.

Drunkenness continues unabated. Relatively little concern is evidenced in the tragic and prodigal tolls of death and carnage on our American highways. Washington's Department of Transportation issued statistics showing that more than 50 percent of the drivers killed in single-vehicle accidents were drunk. Each year 25,000 living Americans become statistics because of alcoholic consumption by drivers and pedestrians. And what about the 800,000 nonfatal traffic accidents due to drinking, leaving in their wake mutilated bodies?

What is behind all this? What is behind all the protest marches? What is prompting the futile search for reality and meaning in life exhibited by the hippies' refusal to accept personal responsibility? Why the lingering, vexing problem of Vietnam, the initial police action which has developed into a continuous inferno reaching into thousands of our homes and threatening to break out in other critical areas?

We ministered in Vietnam and I can tell you it is a sobering experience to look into the face of war, to hear the sound of warfare in the surrounding hills, to see 18- and 19-year-old youths in their prime, going off into a battle that is bloody and brutal, realizing that many will not return.

The men in Vietnam called it the "dirty war," not only from the standpoint of its primitive conditions, but because of the savage tactics employed. We visited the marine medical battalion and witnessed the results of the cruel manner in which young men had been disfigured and dismembered. Viewing the largest military morgue in the world, we shall never forget the bodies of men who had been killed in action being prepared for shipment to the United States.

War is a hideous thing. It is not just the conflict and war tensions of the moment. No, these are just the outward signs of the deep-seated turmoil and chaos in man's spirit today.

Those of you who know this ministry know me to be a man of faith, practicing the optimism of faith. I do not deal in negatives. I think and believe in a positive manner. I believe in America. My roots are here. My Indian heritage declares its allegiance to the land I love. What I am sharing with you is neither an emotional feeling nor an intellectual discourse. It stems from the spirit of urgency that has been placed upon me.

I have been trying to understand why God has quickened my heart so, and stirred the core of my being with the knowledge of the lateness of the hour and of the imminent return of the Lord Jesus Christ. It may be that my time is short. It could be that your time is short. It is possible that America's time is short. It may herald the beginning of apocalyptic judgments. I really do not know. I only know what I feel and I want to cry. I am driven to prayer.

On May 9, 1968, Jesus Christ appeared to me again. As I prayed, I saw before me a deep and wide river that

9

had to be crossed; it seemed the whole human race was on the other side. It was as though the people were hiding in the rocks, stricken with the futility of their own efforts and waiting for God's light to shine on and illuminate their path, waiting to hear His voice and to feel His power delivering them.

I felt the Lord standing in front of me before I saw Him. I said, "Jesus, I want to put my hands in Yours." I saw Jesus take my hands as He held me to Him and poured His presence and strength into me, engulfing me with knowledge for His work. In an instant I was across the river and going throughout the world even to the farthest points, taking the full gospel of Jesus of Nazareth. People surrounded me on all sides. They were crying out from their hiding places, "I see God's light, I hear His voice, I feel His power making me whole."

An overwhelming sense of responsibility swept over me, reaching deep within my inner man. At that moment I knew for certain what I had been feeling for several months, that the Spirit of the Lord was beginning to move over the earth in a way man had not experienced before.

2

Significant signs of the times

WHAT WILL HAPPEN NEXT? Nations are perplexed and men know not which way to turn. Marked uncertainty prevails on every continent and mistrust hampers any real progress at the peace conference tables.

Few realists would deny that the sword of Damocles has been replaced by the mushroom cloud, a constant threat hovering over mankind, threatening its annihilation. Man has a tenfold nuclear capacity to kill every human being on the face of the earth and this awesome record will continue to multiply. Man has successfully orbited the moon, fondly viewing our globe as an oasis in the vastness of space. An oasis for how long? The rumbling of the distant kingdom of the Antichrist is sensed by the sensitive. We are on the eve of something awesome and we can feel it.

Red Russia and Communist China threaten to bury the world, be it by their euphemistic "peaceful coexistence" or by triggering continuous outbreaks of localized wars. The iron fist behind the velvet glove of the Kremlin was exposed to the world in the bloodbath of Hungary in 1956 and the massive invasion of Dubcek's shortlived democratized Czechoslovakia in 1968. Multitudes live under the gnawing dread of a confrontation of the great nuclear powers that will pass the point of no return.

While I was behind the Iron Curtain in Warsaw,

Poland, I conversed at length with the minister of religion. I witnessed to him about God and he responded by lauding Communism. I discovered that the first step in becoming a Christian is, paradoxically, the first step in becoming a Communist! But the second and third steps are radically different.

Christ challenges, "If any man will come after me, let him deny himself" (Matthew 16:24). This is the first step in becoming a Christian — one must turn away from oneself. The second step is to turn toward Christ. The third step taken as a Christian is to turn with Christ toward the world with open and healing hands.

The Communist takes the essential first step: he turns away from self. But for the second step he turns toward the ideology of Communism. And in the third step he turns with the state toward the world, but his hand is closed into a fist to subdue or destroy his fellowman.

In Soviet Russia, I felt a spirit of depression everywhere. I found myself in a completely materialistic state where the existence of God is denied and where the concepts of God are ridiculed. Scientific atheistic propaganda becomes the daily diet of indoctrination for every schoolchild, administered by Soviet teachers trained to wean them from all vestiges of religious "opiates."

In a recent televised documentary film describing Red China, the Red Guard was shown erecting large statues of Mao Tse-tung, almost deifying him. In addition, the Red Guard has exalted his books to the level of the Scriptures.

But what of sophisticated America? Is not God

denied if our confidence rests in our technological knowledge and in our military power? Our acquisitions on national and individual levels are not indicators of our real worth. Spiritual values must receive top priority. Do they?

In a meeting with the president of one of our nation's theological seminaries, I asked, "Don't you agree that the answer for the Body of Christ is to have the gifts of the Holy Spirit in operation again?"

He responded with a very definite, "Yes." Then I queried, "What is keeping the Church from doing this?"

With a most sober expression he looked at me for a moment and then replied, "Reverend Roberts, I agonize over this very thing day and night. Materialism has taken over the people. The Church Militant has become the church hesitant. Theology is a shambles."

Naturalism has crept into Christianity and has eliminated the flow of the supernatural power of God. The glory of the Lord is departing. When you enter the average church today, what do you feel and see and hear? Are you aware that the members have been with Jesus? Do the unregenerate present in a service have the opportunity to find Christ as personal Savior? Is the Holy Spirit honored as the Administrator of His spiritual gifts through individual members in order to edify the entire congregation? Is there prayer for the sick and afflicted, with signs following? Do the lame walk, the blind see, and the deaf hear as in New Testament days, as a result of effectual prayer?

A great percentage of young people who come from a background of regular church attendance and good Christian homes fail to retain their religious convictions in a secular college. They discontinue church attendance and reason that the faith they were raised in is now irrelevant, no longer valid.

My fear is that within my lifetime thousands of churches in America will virtually be emptied. This is the way our country is going. This is part of the great falling away that the Bible prophesied. It is now coming to pass.

The closer we approach the midnight hour of our present civilization the more pronounced will be the sins of our society. Before the judgment of the flood, God saw that the wickedness of man was great in the earth and that every imagination of the thoughts of his heart was only evil continually. The world had reached the climax in its decision to totally reject God. Noah had arrived at a climax in his decision to totally accept God. The climactic decision for both had occurred simultaneously.

God made a pronouncement, saying, "My spirit shall not always strive with man . . . yet his days shall be an hundred and twenty years." God permitted mankind a 120-year period of grace, a more-than-adequate time during which man was given the opportunity to hear and respond to the Word of God.

For decade after decade Noah faithfully obeyed God. He served as a constant warning to the world of coming judgment. Before the 120 years had elapsed, Noah had constructed a huge vessel, an ark large enough to accommodate living pairs that would respond to God. The animals of the fields and forests and the fowls of the air heard God's command and they responded. Then Noah's family entered the ark before God shut the door.

Before the deluge, one priceless week of time, seven

14

last precious days of grace to call upon God were granted but were spurned by the scoffing and rejecting world of unbelievers. Then it started. It began to rain, something it had never done before in the memory of mankind. All the fountains of the great deep burst forth and the windows of heaven were opened. The rain came in driving sheets and covered the ground. It filled the earth and ascended to the highest mountains. And every living thing except those in the ark was destroyed. When enough sin pollutes the earth, a point of saturation is reached. It invited a world flood on that occasion. And the final climax of man's sin shall upset the delicate balance of the groaning creation, thereby releasing a terrible nuclear chain reaction that shall ultimately reduce to ashes every living thing not aligned with God. (Revelation 20:9.)

When the world disregards the conviction of the Holy Spirit and determines to totally reject God, I believe that at that exact time the people of God shall have determined to dedicate themselves totally to God. There will be a simultaneous climax of the persuasion of both the world and God's people. When that occurs, two events will take place.

First, the climax of the dedication of God's people will cause Christ to return. That will be the great day when Jesus will suddenly and secretly return for His own. The climax of the world's rejection of Christ will produce the Antichrist, the False Prophet, the Tribulation, and the destruction of the armies of the world in the Battle of Armageddon.

In receiving inquiries from people all over the world, I am asked repeatedly, "Do you believe in the Second Coming of Jesus Christ? If so, how and when and where shall He return? These answers are to be found in the Scriptures, God's Word. Our omniscient God has known the end from the beginning. Prophecy is history written in advance, and those who diligently study the Bible may expect future events to spread out before their mind's eye in a grand panorama, revealing successive views of the events which must shortly come to pass. What God's prophets have written will be fulfilled.

Jesus, in anticipation of the troublesome events of the end time, had these words of encouragement for His followers, "When these things begin to come to pass, then look up, and lift up your heads; for your redemption draweth nigh" (Luke 21:28).

We are also informed that at the appointed time Antichrist shall appear on the world scene, equipped with man's wisdom and Satanic wisdom with which to wrestle with the problems and dilemmas of the day. He will be heralded as the champion of human rights and will energetically begin to transform the poverty-stricken areas of the world, giving hope to the masses. For a time there will be an abundance of employment and a sound economic guide pointing to financial stability. Rich and poor alike shall be swayed by his magnetic power and shall eagerly follow him before discovering that he is the Antichrist of biblical prophecy.

The question arises, How near are we to Christ's coming, Antichrist's appearance and the horrors of the Great Tribulation? Are there any contemporary signs to indicate that these events are near? Definitely yes. We of this generation are witnessing an accelerated succession of these signs, far more than has any preceding generation. Many have never before appeared on the earth. But we need not be ignorant, for the future is being unveiled by our God and we can be aware of coming events. Let us consider a few.

First, there will be a great increase of knowledge and travel. "But thou, O Daniel, shut up the words, and seal the book, even to the time of the end: many shall run to and fro, and knowledge shall be increased" (Daniel 12:4).

The increase of knowledge in our day is staggering. Last year some 20,000 new books were published in the United States alone. The Apollo 8 spacecraft sent back more than 50,000 bits of information per second, enough to fill a standard encyclopedia in an hour. The new biology is tapping the mysteries of life, regenerating defective organs and conducting heart transplants. Scientists are experimenting with erasing and changing memory as if they were editing a tape recorder. Meanwhile, practical robots that were nonexistent a brief decade ago are working full time in many and diverse industries.

Colleges and universities, beset with sit-ins, riots, and mounting problems, are nevertheless attempting to keep pace with the spiraling number of young people who desire higher education. Many of these secular halls of learning permeate the open minds of the majority of students with naturalism and humanism. Many fine youths, possessing faith in God as they enter, leave as agnostics, ready for the philosophy of the Antichrist.

When I was a child the means of transportation were quite limited. We used to travel by foot or in a wagon along muddy roads, but now high-powered automobiles roar along modern multilaned highways. Monorails and hydrofoils race above the traffic and water at top speeds. Supersonic jets can make weekends in Europe routine for many. Numerous astronauts have orbited our earth at 18,000 miles an hour — 300 miles per minute. We've already forgotten that our spacecraft Mariner 11 closely inspected Venus, a planet 36 million miles from the earth. Space scientists speak of men ferrying to and from hotel-like orbiting spaceships. Geologists will be digging into moon craters in search of evidence leading to the origin of the solar system. Many shall run to and fro, and knowledge shall be increased. Never before have the prophecies of Daniel seemed more contemporary.

Second, "There shall be famines, and pestilences, and earthquakes in divers places" (Matthew 24:7).

Each year there are thousands of earthquakes strong enough to be recorded by seismographs. On the average, 10 are major earthquakes.

In this century we have witnessed death tolls surpassing 200,000 in Kansu, China. In the California earthquake, extending the length of 750 miles, the amount of energy released by this movement exceeded the power of the Hiroshima atomic blast by 100,000 times. More recently, earthquakes leveled 80 percent of Skopje, Yugoslavia, in 1963, and Tashkent, Central Asia, suffered 12 weeks of jolting convulsions wrought by more than 550 quakes in 1966, leaving many killed and 300,000 homeless.

Multiplied millions during my lifetime have perished in widespread famines in India, Russia and China. In 1943, there were 1½ million deaths due to famine in Bengal. Following World War II, 15 million lives were saved from famine by the United Nations Relief and Rehabilitation Administration.

Pestilence follows in the wake of wars and famines. Shortly after World War I an influenza epidemic covered the earth, claiming more than 10 million lives.

Today we are faced with an apocalyptic inventory which man himself may create by littering the sky with radioactive debris whose seepage will infect the earth and plague human tissues. Bacteriological warfare spreading deadly diseases is a dreaded reality in our age. Never before in history has all mankind been lined up to march as sheep to the slaughter.

Third, there will be world perplexity and national distress. Jesus indicated that there would be " . . . distress of nations, with perplexity . . . men's hearts failing them for fear, and for looking after those things which are coming on the earth; for the powers of heaven shall be shaken" (Luke 21:25, 26).

Man now possesses the social, economic, ideological, and scientific power to threaten the world with destruction. The problems are overwhelming and no solutions adequate to the awesome challenge are evident. The stress and strain of the last third of 20th century life are more than many can bear.

Today we have become numbed to terms such as overkill and megadeath. One author suggested that we cease reckoning time by using A.D. and substitute P.H. (Post Hiroshima) and begin with the year 1945. Thus 1970 would be P.H. 25, to daily impress upon minds our radical break with the past, for now one H-bomb can destroy a city. More distressing is the fact that radioactive dust from a cobalt bomb would kill most living beings as it crossed a continent. A nuclear war could be triggered by accident, miscalculation, or madness. Our world offers no sure way, no panacea, no practical program that would prevent men's hearts failing them for fear.

Fourth, there will be strivings for peace, ever elusive. "For when they shall say, Peace and safety; then sudden destruction cometh upon them" (1 Thessalonians 5:3). The United Nations continues to exist only because of man's desperate desire and hope for world peace.

With nations whose minds are full of suspicion, fear and distrust, a continuous climate of hot and cold wars pervades. When a fresh clash erupts, a new arrow pierces the hearts of people everywhere.

By their own definition, Soviet Russia's leaders understand "peaceful coexistence" to mean the prosecution of their offensive toward the goal of world dominion by all means short of general nuclear war which would be suicidal for all concerned.

Some see the nuclear bomb as a blessing in disguise — producing a balance of terror which will prolong an uneasy, fragile peace. Strange that the man who discovered TNT never used it, but instead left a fortune to be awarded each year to individuals who would do the most for the cause of peace in the world. But Alfred Nobel's dream is ever elusive, as attested by the patient diplomats who spend weary months attempting to negotiate peace plans while others strive for nuclear nonproliferation, a meaningful control to prevent atomic stockpiles from becoming the property of smaller nations.

Fifth, there will be an escalation of iniquity. A recent report amounting to almost 2,000 pages listed crimes known to the police — close to 4 million crimes committed in all parts of our nation for one calendar year. Sin continues to abound in ever-increasing measure as the end draws near.

Each year a billion dollars in cash and goods are stolen from companies by their own employees. Graft and corruption in governments are considered normal in many countries.

Films are garishly advertised as lustful sensationalism. Perversion, degeneration, desecration, and violence abound. Even some films using biblical titles are sordid and depraved. Films and TV shows which should not be permitted in the homes are today routine fare for the family. We have been numbed to insensitivity.

There is to be a repetition of the antediluvian and Sodomite conditions in the last days. "And as it was in the days of Noe, so shall it be also in the days of the Son of man. They did eat, they drank, they married wives, they were given in marriage, until the day that Noe entered into the ark, and the flood came, and destroyed them all." (Luke 17:26-30 and Genesis 6:5, 11-13.) To them God was completely ignored, or dead as far as their own plans and desires were concerned, even as He is to a majority of our contemporary society.

Sixth, there will be widespread and increased apostasy. "That day shall not come," said Apostle Paul, "except there come a falling away first, and that man of sin be revealed" (2 Thessalonians 2:3). Many who once believed and adhered to the basic doctrines of God's Word have now turned away from the truth. The Christ of Calvary, the Savior and Healer, has been obscured. Instead, there is a programmed churchianity devoid of vital Christianity, an esthetic form of godliness excluding the energizing power of God, and the letter of the Word which ministers death because it is divorced from the life-giving Spirit of God. Beautiful, finely appointed sanctuaries are not enough; it is essential that the Spirit of Christ inhabit the house and the people of the Lord.

Multiplied thousands have departed from the faith. Other ideologies and philosophies have been substituted for the soundness of salvation. People have hardened their hearts and have turned a deaf ear to the truth. One of the saddest events to witness is a man once aflame for God, but now cold and indifferent. Humanity is faced with an insatiable foe. As a roaring lion he seeks whomever he may devour. Through numerous false prophets Satan is misleading multitudes as he prepares way for acceptance of the Antichrist.

Seventh, we may look for a relevant, Spirit-filled people. I do not believe that men will destroy themselves in this generation. Man will not totally annihilate the human race before the coming of Christ. In spite of his awesome stockpiles of nuclear armaments, he will not destroy himself. There will be other outbreaks and wars, but total annihilation will not be effected by man.

Remember that where sin abounds, the grace of God does much more abound. God is endowing His people with the faith to appropriate His promises. Against destructive nuclear weapons, God's people may have weapons of deliverance — the nine supernatural gifts of the Holy Spirit in full operation.

God is stirring the hearts of His missionary forces in all areas of the world. Mighty miracles will arrest the heathen, initiating a revival the like of which has not been known before in the history of the world.

I have traveled more than 1 million miles to preach the unsearchable riches of Christ, to win souls, and to pray for the healing and wholeness of humanity. Students from Oral Roberts University are stepping into the gap, in ever-increasing numbers in areas of need. God has shown me that there is to be a uniting of the anointed people of God for the final revival. In the hearts of God's people there will be a kindred spirit, drawing each to the other to advance the concluding revival.

Last, but by no means the least of the definite signs of the last days, is the return of the Jews to Palestine. For centuries the descendants of Abraham have been despised, persecuted, and pillaged. Scattered across the nations in diaspora, they have not lost their racial distinctiveness despite the quiet threat of assimilation. They have been hounded by the Pharaohs, the Nebuchadnezzars, the Hamans, and the Hitlers of history, but the Jew has survived. Beyond human comprehension, our century recorded the inhuman slaughter of 6 million Jews under the demonical dictatorship of Hitler, because they were Jews.

Referring to Israel, Jesus said, "Now learn a parable of the fig tree; When his branch is yet tender, and putteth forth leaves, ye know that summer is nigh: So likewise ye, when ye shall see all these things, know that it is near, even at the doors" (Matthew 24:32, 33). Most Bible scholars are in agreement that the budding of the fig tree and the shooting forth of its branches are a type of the Jews returning to their homeland.

Shortly after the atomic era began, the nation of Israel was reborn on May 14, 1948. The dream for which world Jewry had prayed for 19 centuries was at last a reality. The fulfillment of faith and prophecy could no longer be frustrated. The flag of David was raised for the first time since Titus removed it in A.D. 70, when 1 million Jews were slaughtered.

Jerusalem yet remained a divided city for almost 20 years. Then came the dramatic six-day war in June 1967. Unbelievable victory came swiftly. Greater than the military achievement under General Moshe Dayan was the fulfillment of ancient prophecy. One reporter described the entry into the city: "Israeli soldiers were walking about the city as in a dream. Tears rolled down their faces. They did not bother to take cover from Arab snipers. They had realized the 2,000-year-old prophecy of recovering Jerusalem. When they saw the Wailing Wall, they broke out in a dead run until they fell to their knees at the wall. There they sobbed, when victory should have made them exult.

"The mournful bleating of the shofar horn sounded. Unshaven, red-eyed soldiers, their combat uniforms stained with sweat and blood, donned their skullcaps, opened small leather-bound prayer books and rocked back and forth as they chanted, 'Thank the Lord, for the Lord has been kind.' Beyond the wall, heavy firing still could be heard. But the war was forgotten."

Just how important is Israel in the fulfillment of biblical prophecy? How vital are the Israelis to God's timetable? Let us see by now focusing our attention upon these remarkable people.

3

Israel's past in God's timetable

WHEN THE COURT PREACHER was asked by Frederick the Great to supply, in brief, an unanswerable proof for the inspiration of the Bible, he replied, "The Jew, Your Majesty."

Today's proud Israeli stems back to Abraham, a man who made a venture of faith almost 4,000 years ago when he obeyed God's voice instructing him to "Get thee out of thy country . . . unto a land that I will shew thee: And I will make of thee a great nation, and I will bless thee . . . " (Genesis 12:1, 2). This first outstanding figure in the history of Judaism, though imperfect, was a "friend of God" and "the father of the faithful." God has in a special way dealt with and through this ancient nation to bless the world. For this very reason, Satan has constantly made Israel his primary target, ever endeavoring to annihilate the children of Abraham.

Israel, during seasons of rebellion and disobedience to God, experienced suffering exceeding that of other less-enlightened nations. When obedient and faithful, Israel has been exalted above other nations, blessed with God-fearing prophets, priests and kings. Its people are still His people and a providential destiny yet awaits them.

Consider how much we owe this nation. Our precious Bible has come down to us through the Hebrews as the depositories. Never forget that the Lord Jesus

Christ was of Jewish lineage and that Jewish blood flowed in His veins. Peter, James, John, Paul, with all the inspired New Testament writers except Luke the physician, were Jewish. They are the seed of Abraham, beloved for the Father's sake. The Jews have wandered away from God, but His covenant yet remains and will be fulfilled by a faithful remnant. "Have they stumbled that they should fall? God forbid: but rather through their fall salvation is come unto the Gentiles, for to provoke them to jealousy. Now if the fall of them be the riches of the world, and the diminishing of them the riches of the Gentiles; how much more their fulness?" (Romans 11:11, 12). God has not cast away His ancient people, rather He is preparing their hearts for the mass acceptance of Jesus the Messiah at His second advent. The Jews will then believe in Jesus of Nazareth, the only way to salvation for Jew and Gentile alike.

No other race has suffered such unspeakable outrages, impoverishment, racial hatred or frightful persecutions as has the Jewish people. Scattered among the nations — beaten, abused, driven from pillar to post and slaughtered like so many sheep — the Jews have survived to this day. Diabolical schemes have been devised to exterminate them from the face of the earth. The staggering mass executions of one-third of the world's Jews, 6 million human beings, defy description. Cherishing the right to live out their days, they were humiliated, dehumanized, enslaved, starved and tortured before being destroyed in Nazi extermination camps such as Buchenwald, Dachau and Auschwitz.

The dreaded Gestapo spread its dragnet over most of the European Continent under orders of sadistic, insatiably cruel men such as Eichmann. As many as 18,000 Jewish men, women and children were destroyed daily. Think of the confusion and scars in the minds of the Jews asking why the land of Luther had perpetrated such crimes against humanity. Hounded and tormented, the Jews were helpless as their wives and daughters were violated. Their synagogues were sacked and their scrolls, the tablets of the Law, were defiled. Here and there compassionate Europeans risked the wrath of the Nazi secret police in order to protect the Jews. At least 200,000 Jewish refugees were somehow hidden and kept alive in the homes of these unknown heroes or smuggled to safety. In the very shadow of Hitler's headquarters in Berlin, 5,000 Jews remained alive to the war's end. The identical number survived in Warsaw. If ever the need for a national homeland had become acute, the Jews felt it deeply at this time. If ever world sympathy was awakened and world conscience aroused to favor arrangements for the hounded Jewish people to possess a homeland, it was during World War II. Out of unspeakable evil arose the good.

Isaiah prophesied that God would "assemble the outcasts of Israel, and gather together the dispersed of Judah from the four corners of the earth" (Isaiah 11:12). The God of Abraham also declared, "I will plant them upon their land, and they shall no more be pulled up out of their land which I have given them" (Amos 9:14, 15). Now, at last, the outcasts were to return to their homeland, Palestine.

Why Palestine? Why this strange and sacred little corner of the earth? Because the Creator and Landlord of the Universe gave it to them. Palestine is situated at a point of unusual geographic, historic and political interest — past, present and future. It has been called the crossroads of the nations. As a narrow strip of coast along the eastern end of the Mediterranean Sea, it is a link between the Arabian Peninsula on one side, and Asia Minor on the other. By virtue of this strategic location it has been the highway and the bridge between the most ancient seats of civilization. A station on the great lanes of international traffic, Israel is the most central and promising property on earth. God selected this land to be the home of Abraham's offspring.

Palestine was once a land flowing with milk and honey, satisfying a population of more than 3 million. In A.D. 70, Titus and his Roman army besieged Jerusalem, destroyed the temple and slaughtered hundreds of thousands of Israelites. It required six decades to wipe out all pockets of resistance and the people of Israel dispersed in all directions. Throughout the long centuries of Christian history, the Jews were taught to distrust and hate Christianity as they experienced the Frankish Crusades, the Spanish Inquisition, the ghettos and pograms of Europe.

At the close of the 19th century, amidst fiery new outbreaks of anti-Semitism, European Jews again experienced a deep longing for the Holy Land. Several thousand left Eastern Europe, leaving its scars of rejection and wounds of persecution behind, in order to join a nucleus of 25,000 Jews who were then living in Palestine. Shortly thereafter, Theodor Herzl spearheaded the Zionist movement in order to secure for world Jewry, by public law, a home in Palestine. Great Britain, in gratitude to the ingenious discovery of the noted Jewish chemist, Dr. Chaim Weizmann, pledged its aid in behalf of establishing Palestine as an official Jewish state. This was publicized in the Balfour Declaration of 1917, a time when the population of Jews in Palestine had increased to 75,000.

Then came the thrilling report of General Allenby's capture of the Holy City on December 11, 1917. Without firing a shot, Jerusalem was delivered from the fleeing Turks. Without fanfare, Gen. Edmund Allenby, Commander in Chief of the Allied Armies in the East, quietly entered the city of Jerusalem.

Under the four-century reign of the Turks and the preceding centuries of rule by nomadic Arabs, the once-beautiful and fertile land of Palestine had become barren and desolate. When the League of Nations effected a British mandate over Palestine in 1923, thousands of Jewish people prepared to pour into Palestine. Leaders of Zionism negotiated with Arab rulers and purchased poor, unproductive land from Arab owners at a price far exceeding its value. Jewish immigration continued to increase, especially as Hitler's ominous shadow began to fall across Europe. During World War II, the Palestinian Jewish population exceeded 500,000 diligent laborers bent on making the land productive. Upon witnessing the transformation of the barren land, the Arabs who voluntarily sold the land to the Jews demanded its return.

Both Semitic offsprings of Abraham, the Arabs descended from Ishmael while the Jews are descendants of Isaac. God promised to make of Ishmael a great nation (Genesis 17:20), but with Isaac and his seed God was to establish the everlasting covenant. (Genesis 17:19.) This suggests that there was room enough for both to prosper and be great, but bitter strife has

29

existed and does now exist between the Arabs and the Jews, causing a continuous Middle East crisis.

During World War II, the Zionists cooperated fully with the Allies against the hated fascist enemy. Thousands of Jewish soldiers were recruited and entire Jewish units served with the British in several campaigns. In Europe, however, they had no such opportunities. The Nazis successfully exploited the traditional anti-Semitism of the peasants in Eastern Europe so that no aid would reach the Jews. Their extermination was systematically continued in the major death camps of Poland under the fanatically efficient supervision of Eichmann. Brave Jewish uprisings were attempted against overwhelming odds. Thousands of Jewish youths were able to join the various underground resistance movements.

The successful blitzkrieg warfare of the Nazis placed England in a vulnerable position as the German Army was preparing for invasion via the English Channel. Instead, Hitler opened a second front and poured many divisions into the Soviet Union. They rapidly reached the very edges of Russia's largest cities. Then history repeated itself as the turning tide of defeats caused the German armies to retreat as did Napoleon's French armies more than a century before. D-Day witnessed the successful invasion of France by the Allies, who drove the Wehrmacht back into Germany. Finally, following Hitler's suicide, the German warlords signed an unconditional surrender on V-E Day, May 6, 1945.

Hitler's slaughter of 6 million Jews aroused worldwide sympathy and compassion for the Jewish people. It became imperative that Israel have its own homeland to which the scattered, unwanted refugees could go. World Jewry had been reduced from 17 million in 1939, to 11 million in 1945. But God brought good out of this terrible evil. Favorable events shaped rapidly as the problem of Palestine was placed before the newly formed United Nations. By the fall of 1947, the United Nations General Assembly had adopted a majority recommendation to divide Palestine into a Jewish state and an Arab state. The British mandate was to end in six months.

On May 14, 1948, as the last British soldier departed from Palestine, and the Jewish National Council and the Zionist Council at Tel Aviv proclaimed the establishment of the Jewish State of Israel. At last, the despised, dispersed Jewish people were able to return home after 19 centuries of global wanderings. The greatest march to the Holy Land since the days of Moses now began. The new nation of Israel opened its arms to Jews the world around, offering them the right of immigration as all restrictions were abolished to the exiles.

Under the leadership of its first President, Dr. Chaim Weizmann, and Prime Minister David Ben-Gurion, the infant nation Israel beheld the flag of David unfurled over the Holy Land for the first time since Titus removed it in A.D. 70. Many observers feared that the new state would never survive the conditions of bankruptcy, war and the encirclement of hostile Arab nations, yet Israel has sustained every trial against unbelievable odds.

It has been my privilege to research the growth and changes of Israel personally during five visits to the Holy Land. I interviewed its leaders and conversed with people who have converged upon Israel from almost a hundred nations. To each I asked the questions, "Why did you come to Israel? Have you come to meet the Messiah?"

Each time I step upon the soil of Israel there is a feeling akin to awe that sweeps over me. My entire being seems to vibrate with the presence of God. Viewing the people as they plant and rebuild the land makes me realize that I am at grips with a miracle. I see, hear and feel the mighty works that God is accomplishing in that tiny land on the edge of man's wilderness.

The people made a tremendous impact upon my spirit. They have stopped running — they have come home! Now they are possessing the land again in the same manner and spirit of Joshua, foot by foot, hill by hill, town by town. This is the spirit of the land of Israel and I have been drawn irresistibly under its spell.

For about 1,500 years the name of Jesus was seldom mentioned among the Jews and few Jewish writers dealt with Him. But a great change is taking place as Jewish scholars in the United States, Great Britain and Israel have written at length concerning Jesus of Nazareth, so that there is an increasing recognition of Him as a great religious teacher by prominent Jews in the world. It is evident that God is at work among the Jewish people in an effort to prepare them for the reception of Jesus Christ as their Messiah.

From the moment we were greeted by an important government official at the Lydda airport until my first interview with Ben-Gurion, the hand of the Lord was upon our early mission. Extraordinary results were realized, for which I give God all the glory. No Christian minister could enter a country like Israel and enjoy the privileges accorded our group without the help of God. Though cordial and friendly to Christians, and even acknowledging Jesus as a prophet, Israel does not accept Jesus as the Messiah, the Son of God.

A great spiritual experience awaited me at Capernaum in a subsequent visit. In picturesque Capernaum, situated on the northern rim of the Sea of Galilee, I had the privilege of preaching to more than 100 Jews who came to hear me. They had embarked at Tiberias to sail across the sea much as the people did to hear Jesus nearly 2,000 years ago. It was a moving experience to see them leave the vessel and walk through the trees toward the remains of the synagogue in which Jesus preached and healed. My heart was full of Jesus as I eagerly shared with them the great miracles wrought by Him in that sacred place.

A great anointing was upon me as I pointed to the ruins and read Jesus' prophecy: "And thou, Capernaum, which are exalted unto heaven, shalt be brought down to hell: for if the mighty works, which have been done in thee, had been done in Sodom, it would have remained until this day. But I say unto you, That it shall be more tolerable for the land of Sodom in the day of judgment, than for thee" (Matthew 11:23, 24).

"This scene of desolation," I declared, "is a reminder to every living human being to respect the visitation of God. We, too, will find our houses, our cities, our souls left desolate if we do not open our hearts to God's visitation."

I do not know how to describe it, but that crowd of Israelis received my message. One woman who had emigrated from Russia said, "Reverend Roberts, we don't accept Jesus as you do, but we know Jesus loved the people."

As I think back to 1953, I remember seeing very few large trees in Israel. Now there are thousands of acres of virtual forests, and beautiful. Annually, millions of new trees are being planted, principally by the children. They are being taught by their parents to love the land of Israel. As I participated in the process of planting a banana tree I seemed not only to capture the spirit of Israel, but actually to become possessed by it. I was made acutely aware of the deep, moving forces, the human forces of faith, confidence and expectancy.

When a tree is planted, faith in the future is implied. And the Israelis believe confidently and joyously in the future. Many of them realize that they may not live to enjoy these blessings for themselves, but they are building for tomorrow — pouring all of their love, knowledge and understanding into the hearts and minds of their children.

In one communal farm, (the term used is kibbutz), I spoke to a brilliantly educated young American and his wife. Receiving but a fraction of the salary he could have been earning in the United States, the young American was experiencing a greater reward and fulfillment as he helped to train some of the hundreds of thousands of children registered in Israeli schools. Dwelling in a sparsely furnished room, the young teacher was an example of many instructors giving themselves untiringly to their task, yet he exhibited deep satisfaction and joy.

I spent quite some time with this friendly and responsive young man. "Do you look for the Messiah?" I asked.

"I am not religious," he answered. I soon learned that his response meant he was not of the Orthodox Jewish faith. He was not a strict adherent of the Talmud, a collection of Jewish traditions.

"Do you believe in miracles?" I queried.

"No," he responded. He did not believe that the Red Sea had parted for Moses, nor that the walls of Jericho had fallen miraculously. He believed in the miracles of science and the miracle of the rebirth of his nation.

He continued, "But these are miracles we create with our hands. We work in the fields, drive big tractors, plant and cultivate. We harvest and transform our land. The women work alongside the men. And these are things we believe in."

"May I give you my testimony?" I asked.

Politely, but with cautious and reserved eyes, he said, "Please do."

I shared how desperately ill I had been, and how God had saved me and healed me of tuberculosis and a stammering tongue. I related how God had spoken to me and had called me to preach the Good News and to take the message of His healing power to my generation.

He listened quietly, then more intently, until finally he seemed to be hanging upon every word I uttered.

"Do you believe me?" I asked.

"Yes, I do!" he exclaimed as he began to open up. I realized that God had touched his heart.

This couple lived in a kibbutz called Ein Gev, a settlement where about 500 families from 50 countries labored in the fields together, sharing meals together, and placing all their earnings into one treasury. There are many kibbutzim in Israel where people live closely together, sharing mutual interests.

During the earlier fighting, almost every building in this kibbutz was destroyed, but the occupants simply moved underground and continued working. They constructed underground shelters for their families with kitchens, beds and belongings. This was to be their home for six months as the farmer-fighters slipped out to farm during the day and crawled back at night for rest and shelter.

As I looked around me I could understand what the young teacher meant. These Israelis were not afraid. Their faith was unshakable; they believed in their future; they knew they were going to succeed.

As I journeyed across Israel I was impressed with the health and general well-being of the Jewish people. Meeting one of the world's famous physicians, I asked, "Dr. Mann, how do you account for the good health of the Jewish people?"

This eminent doctor, discoverer of the cure for silicosis (a lung disease which afflicts miners), smiled proudly as he replied, "Reverend Roberts, it is truly remarkable. As you know, these people came from everywhere. Once, more than 5,000 suffering from infectious tuberculosis were brought in at one time. I was truly frightened. I didn't know what to do. But the strangest thing took place. The very moment these people set foot on the soil of Israel something happened inside them. They began to get well quickly. Our doctors and our nurses moved into their tents and worked with them, showering their love and attention upon them. The people responded. I almost believe they would have recovered without treatment. Today, we have only 800 bed patients in all of Israel with tuberculosis. My answer is 'I believe God did it!' "

"Dr. Mann, do you believe that God heals?" I asked.

"I most certainly do," he promptly replied, "and I believe almost every doctor will tell you the same thing. I believe God heals because I have seen it with my own eyes."

It was a marked privilege to interview Dr. Mann for he supervised the staff of Hebrew University-Hadassah Medical School, Israel's new $20-million institution which graduates a hundred doctors each year to expand the work of mercy and medical care in Israel.

Among the memorable events of this earlier journey to Israel was a visit with some Yemenite Jews. They arrived from Yemen, located at the southern extremity of Arabia, on the Red Sea. They are believed to have migrated there in King Solomon's day. For these thousands of years they have lived in Yemen, completely cut off from the outside world. Before their exodus to Israel in 1948, they had never seen modern conveniences — no automobiles, trains, planes, electric lights — not even water faucets.

Throughout the centuries they have suffered great persecution, but they have retained the purity of their religion. I conversed with Yemenites who informed me that they had copied the Bible exactly as the people did in Jesus' day, by hand. If any errors were committed in transcribing the Old Testament Scriptures from Genesis to Malachi, the portion would be started once again. Deprived of educational opportunities and facilities, many received their education by memorizing the entire Old Testament.

This isolation of the Yemenite Jews terminated in 1948, at which time God spoke to their leaders and caused them to organize an exodus from Arabia to Palestine. Prime Minister David Ben-Gurion successfully interceded on their behalf, calling upon the United States Government to provide cargo planes. These were dispatched to the British-controlled port of Aden as the rendezvous point from which the Yemenites would be flown to their ancient homeland. But the only way to reach the Aden was to walk — so they walked! Some of them walked 1,000 miles over deserts and mountains, traveling in scorching heat as high as 120 degrees down to freezing temperatures.

The Israeli Government scheduled film crews to film this great exodus and pilgrimage. As I viewed this recorded event, both disturbing and heroic scenes were projected before me. Some died and were buried. Little children were crying for water. The pilgrims stumbled on, and some fell, but one could hear the rabbis encouraging them in strangely vibrant tones, "Take another step, Little Children. We are going home to meet Messiah." Somehow they dragged one foot in front of the other and stumbled on and on.

Mr. Ben-Gurion sent his officials to announce the fact that aircraft were being sent to fly them to the Holy Land. But the Yemenites did not know what an airplane was. When they caught sight of the planes they refused to board them. Not until their rabbis read from the Scriptures, "I bare you on eagles' wings, and brought you unto myself" (Exodus 19:4), and explained that God was sending His eagles for His children, did the Yemenite Jews fearlessly board the planes. Some of the women gave birth to their babies while in flight, but not a single child was lost. The number of Yemenites flown to Israel in this great airlift exceeded 50,000!

Upon landing in Israel, some of the passengers unashamedly kissed the ground. After the authorities placed them on the waiting buses, they expected the buses to fly. Having never seen a bus before, they were disappointed. But they had come home.

I visited the home of a Yemenite family. The yard was filled with happy, friendly little children. The entire neighborhood was there. We went into the kitchen and sat around a table covered with the most beautiful tablecloth I have ever seen. One of the sons translated for his father, an 85-year-old rabbi. Behind his long beard was a very kind face and his eyes were flashing.

I said, "Ask him what his dream is — what he wants most in the world."

The aged rabbi answered in Hebrew saying, "I want three things: first, I want to see Israel developed; second, I want to live long enough to see peace; third, I want to see Messiah with my own eyes."

4

Contemporary Israel in God's timetable

I WAS LOOKING FORWARD to my first interview with David Ben-Gurion with great anticipation. My appointment with Israel's prime minister was for 9:30 a.m., but I was unable to see him until 5 p.m. Several other appointments had been canceled that day because of a political crisis, but the officials assured me of my welcome as a guest of the Israeli Government as they sat with me through the day. Mr. Ben-Gurion graciously received me as I entered his office but I was surprised at the first question he asked. "Mr. Roberts, as a Christian evangelist, what are you trying to do with people? I do not mean what are you trying to get them to believe, but what are you trying to get them to be and to do?"

He is a little man, perhaps no more than 5 feet 3 inches tall, with hair completely white and standing out stiffly. His eyes were luminous and his hands and face wonderfully expressive. His glance was penetrating, as if he were able to read my thoughts. Although unprepared for his question, I received this answer from the Lord before I could really think about it: "I am trying to get people to love one another. I am teaching people that they cannot love God without also loving their fellowman."

Mr. Ben-Gurion smiled as he said, "Mr. Roberts, that's a good answer. But love is not enough. People have needs. There can be no equality among people until those needs are met. Do you agree?"

"Yes," I said. "I believe that love must be translated into action. That is what Jesus taught."

"That's right," he agreed.

We discussed human needs and people who lacked decent housing, adequate clothing, and sufficient food. He continued, "Love becomes an empty word unless you meet the needs of these people."

I agreed, saying, "Yes, I believe God comes to meet the needs of people. He comes in the form of their needs."

Later, when he declared Israel's love for the Bible, I posed this question, "Mr. Ben-Gurion, what has the Bible had to with the rebirth of Israel?"

"Everything!" was his ready response. "Without the Bible we could have done nothing. The Bible said we would return to this land. We have come home. The Bible said we would rebuild the land. We are rebuilding it. The Bible said we would plant the land. We are planting it."

I could verify this for I had been all over the land, seeing it blossoming like the rose. For this reason almost 1½ million Jewish people were able to return to this land in its first 15 years as an independent nation. Soon Israel will be accommodating a population of 3 million.

I then presented the prime minister with one of our Bibles, containing both Old and New Testaments in the Hebrew language, saying, "Would you accept this as a token of the love of the Christian people who also love Israel?"

"Mr. Roberts, I will be very proud to have it."

Inside the beautiful white-covered copy I wrote the inscription, "May the blessing of the Bible be upon you, Mr. Prime Minister, and upon the people of Israel."

He read to me from the Hebrew Bible and then it was time for my departure. My last question was, "Mr. Ben-Gurion, what is your dream for Israel?"

Almost spontaneously came this response, "I want Israel to be an example to other nations of love, freedom and dedication. And I want Israel to be as the Prophet Jeremiah says, 'a light to all nations.' "

I then prayed with the prime minister and took my leave. Thus ended the most memorable event of this visit to Israel, whose government had proved a most gracious host.

Wherever I journeyed in Israel I found our Hebrew Bibles. In schools, in libraries, in the Hebrew University, and in homes, the Bibles were to be found everywhere. Our Evangelistic Association has printed the complete Bible in Hebrew and more than 100,000 of them have been distributed in the Holy Land during the past 15 years. Jews will not listen to the usual preaching but they will read these Bibles printed in pure Hebrew. The language has been restored to popular usage and the Old Testament is taught in the public schools and universities. The New Testament is read as religious literature, even though it is not considered on the same level as the Old Testament by Orthodox Jews. The person of Jesus still disturbs the searching hearts among the Israelis. Others, less concerned, may not read these Bibles for months or even years, but God's time will arrive. And when it does, thousands of Jews will avidly read the Bibles which have remained unread in their homes. The Holy Spirit will then reveal Jesus to them as their true Messiah.

During the summer of 1968, an Oral Roberts University World Action Team flew to Israel. Everybody was excited to be entering the Holy Land, most for their first time. When we landed, the Israeli Government had representatives officially to welcome us with beautiful red roses. The press took pictures and the airport authorities got us quickly through customs without opening our bags.

At the airport terminal our World Action Team sang, in both Hebrew and English, and a crowd quickly gathered and burst into applause. They were smiling and clapping and looking at one another with delight. "Who is it?" they asked. As I watched I praised God for giving me such a team of fearless workers who are proud of Jesus and who enlarge my endeavors to reach the people.

What remarkable changes since my first visit in 1953! The land is no longer barren. The people have planted 85 million trees and the land is under cultivation and irrigation everywhere. Orthodox Jews mingle with the Jews who have little or no faith but they are all busy working the land, building cities and establishing the nation. The winding road which the Arabs had closed was now open and we saved five miles going to Jerusalem.

Jerusalem — what changes there! A lump always comes in my throat when I see Jerusalem, although this was my fifth visit. Gone are the dividing walls, the barbed wire separating the ancient city is not there and the city is united again for the first time since A.D. 70! I could tell by my guide's reactions that there is a different feeling here. A prophetic element is gripping the people. Our task for the next two weeks was to witness about the Man they believe to have been a prophet only but who we know is the Son of the living God. This is an exciting hour. Anything can happen.

I began writing the next day at 5 o'clock in the morning. The sun was up and streaming over Jerusalem. From my hotel window on Mount Olivet, Jerusalem spread before my gaze. The eastern wall was before me and I remembered the Scripture, "Pray for the peace of Jerusalem."

I slipped from the room and went out and sat on the side of Mount Olivet. For several minutes I just sat there before the Lord. After a while, the Holy Spirit began to move through my soul and body. I could feel Jesus' hands upon me, bidding me to pray. I broke into tongues, praising the Lord and magnifying His name. All at once I heard myself saying, "The precious blood of Jesus covers my soul this morning, the blood that was shed right over there outside the wall of the city. All my sins are under that blood and I am washed whiter than snow. My soul is baptized with the Holy Spirit and here I sit speaking in tongues within a few hundred yards of the Upper Room where on Pentecost morning Jesus baptized the disciples and His mother and they spoke in tongues and glorified God. I am healed of tuberculosis and stuttering which I had as a boy, by the same Savior who healed the impotent man at the Pool of Bethesda, only a few paces from here. I am a witness to Jesus near the same spot where He said, "And ye shall be witnesses unto me . . . in Jerusalem and in all Judaea, and in Samaria, and unto the uttermost part of the earth" (Acts 1:8).

The sun shining over Jerusalem was like a blinding

floodlight, so bright it burned my eyes. I heard Malachi say, "The sun of righteousness rises with healing in His wings." Again I was enveloped by Jesus, my heart bursting in gratitude, feeling like running and running and shouting to the whole human race, "Jesus is coming! Jesus is coming! Get ready while there's still time left!"

There is an entirely different spirit in Israel since the six-day war in 1967. Each time I have been in Israel I have felt the moving of God's Spirit in the land. I say "in the land" in the sense that the people have put their hands to it and it has come alive and is being renewed: the desert is blossoming as the rose. I had a feeling that the people, with few exceptions, had returned and were doing all these things as a direct result of prophecy but were not aware of just why they were doing them. They felt a powerful force, an inner urge, but without coming into a personal confrontation with God.

The results of the six-day war both lifted their spirits to new heights and brought soberness to them. They now have the land from the Suez to the Jordan. Jerusalem is united for the first time in almost 2,000 years. Gone are the barriers dividing the city and the land. The Wailing Wall, the only remaining part of the Temple of Ezra and later added to by King Herod, is in the hands of the Jews, and daily they are there making their bitter cry, "Come, Messiah. Come, Messiah."

Some miracles happened there during this war, things that have made the Jews think on God. For example, in Nablus (ancient Samaria, where Jesus met the woman at the well), the entrance to the city had been heavily mined from all directions except the south, where the terrain was so rough it was thought the Israelis could not enter. But that was exactly the way they brought the tanks in. The people in the city thought the tanks belonged to their own army and met them with great rejoicing. They surrendered the city without the firing of a shot. It took the minds of the Jews back to Bible times and it became the talk of the country.

The first night on the campus of Hebrew University reflected the new mood of faith and deeper religious thought in Israel. Sponsored by a very warm friend of this ministry, the Honorable Teddy Kolleck, Mayor of Jerusalem, the program in Wise Auditorium drew people from all walks of life in the city, including those involved in government, business and education. The songs about the Lord, about all nations joining together to worship God, made a terrific impact. Even when the team sang "Ye Are My Witnesses" there was prolonged applause. My own message was well received. For an hour and a half the ORU students sang, witnessed, and gave all they had for the Lord. Instead of reaction, which would have happened before the six-day war, everything we did of a spiritual nature caused a deep response.

Afterward, the mayor hosted a reception and conveyed his appreciation for our coming. We joined hands with him and other leaders and had prayer together. I felt like pinching myself. Is this really happening in Israel? Have we actually been given this open door to witness of our Savior? I recalled God's message when He had told us to go into "all nations" and I had said, "How, Lord?"

He had said, "By My Spirit."

This has certainly begun to happen. God's Spirit is opening the doors.

Mayor Teddy Kolleck said, "Reverend Roberts, when the news of what we heard and felt in our hearts tonight is carried by the press over Israel, you will not be able to seat the crowds during the rest of your tour." Then he said, "Instead of several hundred, as on this first night, when you return to Jerusalem in the future, I feel we can take the stadium which seats 17,000 and pack it out."

Thank God, thank God! It's taken a long time for Israel to get ready for this, and for us to have a team of exceptional talent and dedication to witnessing, but it's happening. I thought, "I can't wait to see what the Lord will do tomorrow as we go into Galilee."

As we go into Galilee! It seemed natural for me to say it. I wonder how many times Jesus said it to His disciples?

At the Ein Gev Kibbutzim on the Sea of Galilee, Mayor Kolleck helped start this cooperative community and it was he who arranged for our meeting. A delicious supper of fish caught that day in the Sea of Galilee was awaiting us in the dining room by the edge of the sea. I think all of us were thinking of Jesus as He said to the disciples who had fished all night and taken nothing, "Cast your net on the right side," and they "enclosed a multitude of fishes." In a few minutes we would be offering the people who lived around the sea another kind of supper; the Word of the Lord in music, song, testimony, and hearts full of love and faith.

As we entered the amphitheater we heard the sound of artillery in the distance. Just that morning a young girl had been injured on a nearby farm from such fire.

I talked with the team a few moments about the dangers in this land. However, 2,000 years ago Jesus faced dangers that were just as real to Him then as those we faced. The Sea of Galilee was rolling high only a few feet from the stage; the winds had been strong ever since we had arrived hours earlier. Our voyage to the kibbutzim had been canceled because of the waves. Angry waves and angry artillery were all about us. In our devotions by the water's edge we put these from our minds and gave ourselves to Jesus. We could really feel His presence.

The meeting began at 9 p.m. to allow the people time to finish their farm chores and eat. Right up to starting time there was hardly anyone there. Then within 15 minutes, 1,400 had arrived! Military ambulances rolled in near the stage "just in case," I was told, "a shell strikes here or we are attacked." Our World Action students looked at each other; it was serious business, yet everyone was excited and thrilled to be there.

Looking out over the audience I realized their task was the same as in the Exodus, to take the land, to make it blossom as the rose, to exercise the same fierce determination and faith to restore the nation. Some know why they have returned, some do not, but they all recognize something here greater than themselves and what they are doing is something they have to do. Much suffering lies ahead before they will be ready to know our Savior. Right now they are locked in battle with the land, with the world around them which would deny their existence. The audience that evening was predominantly composed of young people. Soldiers, both young men and women, were there in numbers.

A few older people were scattered among the crowd.

We were under the stars. Behind us was the Sea of Galilee. Before us were 1,400 Israelis. In our hearts we felt the Man of Galilee. "O come, let us sing of His glory. Come all nations into one congregation. Bring a song from every shore unto the Lord." My spine tingled as the group sang these words, their trumpets sounding, their voices blending, their spirits lifting, and their joy in the Lord going out to the people before them. Never before had a Christian group like this sung in Israel.

We journeyed on north of the Sea of Galilee to the Upper Galilean Valley which the Jews have made into a beautiful area of orange groves, vegetables, and fish hatcheries. For 20 years it has been under the guns of a hill on the Syrian side. It was the one most dangerous place for the Israelis to live and work in. Whoever controlled this hill controlled the entire valley. In the six-day war it was taken at the cost of many lives and the guns were silenced.

How did they take it? "By a miracle," we were told. The whole area was completely mined, yet in a few hours Israeli soldiers stormed the hill and took it. They found soldiers chained to the guns so they would not run away.

We were on our way to the Golan Hills to perform at El Kuneitra, just a couple of miles from the Syrian border. These are the hills of Elijah. We had to stop at various military checkpoints, which reminded me that in the past two summers the Lord had sent me to two major war areas in the world, Vietnam and the Middle East. Of the two areas, this one is believed to be the more explosive as far as world peace is concerned. My own view is a biblical one. "There shall be wars and rumors of wars," said Jesus when He was there. If Jesus tarries, many more wars will plague a world that continues to reject God.

El Kuneitra, Syria, was a deserted city occupied by the Israeli Army. The terrain is quite like the area we were in near Da Nang, Vietnam — hot, dusty, and with the feel of war on it. Great care was taken with us, for thousands of mines are still in the area. The Syrians fired on the city nearly every night, and checkpoints were located every few hundred yards. We got through safely and were received by the leaders in the mess hall where a meal was served to us. "Can you eat what our soldiers eat?" I was asked. "If they can eat it, we can, too," I replied. And we did.

This is a raw, primitive area directly on the frontier, exactly where the United Nations stopped the war. In another day or two, probably all of Syria would have fallen. Signs said "Frontier Ahead," meaning "No Man's Land." One's life was in danger here every moment.

The major said, "Reverend Roberts, you won't be able to seat all our personnel. No group like yours has been here before." We used the theater building and I was unprepared for what happened there that evening. The soldiers came directly from the front lines and the entire area, guns in hand. The officers kept moving about in the audience, never sitting in one place very long. Outside, the building was under heavy guard.

Our team was equal to it. The piano had been blown apart in the war, so we did without it. When they finished their first song, pandemonium broke out.

I'd never before heard such applause. "More! More!" they clamored. Our chief witness song was "I've Discovered the Way of Gladness." There were key phrases such as "I've found Jesus" and "I've accepted His sacrifice."

There was a little trepidation as we sang this one. These soldiers were tough; you could feel the spirit that possesses and drives them to recapture their homeland. There was raw power in the theater that evening; 16 submachine guns were counted in one section alone.

You can't know Israel at this time without seeing her soldiers. There is no safety anywhere in the land. The people live under the protest of the nations surrounding them. They are willing to fight to the death to stay there: "We'll never give up this land. We've been driven here from centuries of homelessness from more than 70 nations. We've no place to go. This is our home." This was said quietly, with no rancor. But you felt the words biting into your flesh and spirit. You knew it was so.

As we neared the end of the program the soldiers sensed it and sent word that if we didn't give them more they would remove the wheels from our bus! Believe me, we complied. Finally the Hebrew M.C. said, "Enough! Enough!" and got us through our final encore, which was "Jerusalem the Gold." What a beautiful song this is, and sung by our students feeling the impact of Israel upon them and the spirit of being witnesses unto Jesus among His ancient people, it can break you up. It was especially moving to these people who see Jerusalem now united, the symbol of all their centuries-old hopes.

Later, under military escort, with heavy machine

guns mounted on each vehicle before us and behind us, we drove through the night out of the Golan Hills military area. The escort left us as we entered Galilee.

The next day we were in Tel Aviv to appear on Radio Israel in a meeting where 900 people were present. As we came into the hall where the broadcast was to be made, we were told that the officer in charge had called our director and said, "Now this is the kind of program we want you to send us." The world is ready for Holy Spirit-filled young people who are trained, who are sold out to Christ, and who are ready to be missionary Christians. I feel that if these tough Israeli soldiers respond, people will respond everywhere.

All the students were ecstatic. So was I. God was doing something. For 15 years I have been going to Israel, with no opportunity for me, or anyone, including the missionaries, to make a real witness in Israel. But God has given me friends there in high places. At last when I could go with 36 young men and women, highly gifted and trained and willing to face the situation as it was, with a repertoire of songs that people could relate to, then I found the door open.

In my fondest hopes for this trip I did not include Radio Israel, and especially on the evening before their Sabbath (like our Saturday night in the United States) when the entire nation would be listening. Our World Action young people were introduced to a packed studio audience, and for a solid hour they communicated.

To the listeners we were a group of Christians from America giving them top entertainment; to ourselves we were missionary Christians releasing the love of

Jesus of Nazareth. At the midpoint of every performance was a testimony of a student, a Christ-centered
song, and above all, the witness of the students themselves, their faces radiant with Christ's love.

That evening I was asked to participate. This was
a time when, as president of a university, having a
group of students with me, I was able to give a nationwide witness to Israel. Without this team I could not
have spoken to large audiences in person and now to
hundreds of thousands at prime listening time over
Radio Israel. And without the 15 years during which
Dr. Myron Sackett and I worked in this land, beginning
with the government leaders, the students could not
have had this open door.

On Radio Israel, in the midst of the program I was
presented and this is part of what I said:

"Shalom, Men and Women of Israel. I bring you
greetings from Christians in America who love you and
are praying for you. The group you are hearing tonight
is a World Action Team here to testify of the Lord, the
same Lord who has brought you here, the God of Abraham, Isaac and Jacob. And now let me share something of what I feel concerning Israel and Jerusalem.

"Like a diamond on a velvet couch the city of Jerusalem is situated in the geographical center of the earth.
It is the city of God the great King. Here He sent His
prophets, here His law went out to the ends of the
earth.

"In 586 B.C. Nebuchadnezzar came with his con-
quering legions, burned and rocked the city and took
captive the flower of the nation as trophies of his
victory. He tried to defeat God, to destroy the spirit of
His people. But in Babylon when he tried to force

them to bow to his image of gold, they refused, and turning their faces toward Jerusalem, they cried, 'O Jerusalem, O Jerusalem, if I forget thee let my right hand forget its cunning . . . let my tongue cleave to the roof of my mouth.'

"Through the centuries since A.D. 70 and the destruction of Jerusalem by the Roman general Titus, your people have wandered over the world, always remembering Jerusalem. Now God has called, you have heard His voice once again, saying, 'Take another step, Little Children, you are going home.'

"You are here rebuilding the land. A year ago you took all of Jerusalem and for the first time in 2,000 years Jerusalem is united. Gone are the physical barriers separating itself and God's people and it is a whole city again. (Applause.)

"For me, for us who are committed Christians, the Messiah has already come; for you He is yet to come. We believe it is no accident that you and we are meeting in this way tonight here in the auditorium and over Radio Israel.

"We are praying for you and we say, God bless you."

Again there was heavy applause and I believe it was heartfelt. I don't mean to imply that their response was indicative of a sudden change toward Jesus. I do believe it was the first nationwide witness of this type and that God placed us here to give it as part of His call to "go to all nations."

Our program over Radio Israel was used on two successive Friday evenings. In my prayers I have reminded Jesus of His Word as He sent it forth, bearing thirtyfold, sixtyfold and a hundredfold, and prayed that what we have done there will bring forth a hundredfold. It is our task to witness; it's His to multiply it.

God had given us a plan, unlike the typical ones used by Christian organizations which have tried hard in Israel. The Jews are a cultured people, they love music, they love their young people, and just as any other people they respond to those who respect and love them. Through the years we had done certain things to reveal our true feelings for Israel. We kept our contacts in the government there and in the United States. We selected 36 of our top students and formed them into a band and choral group, trained them in a rigorous program of discipline and witnessing. They were going into battle, we told them, using many different weapons such as music, but to be alert for that moment when they would be in a position to witness. "Be wise as serpents," we reminded them of Jesus' words, "and harmless as doves."

By personal experience I know the formidable difficulties of witnessing in Israel.

How wise God is. He moves one step at a time. I have known men, godly men, who have gone to Israel with a great vision to win the people to Christ. But they treated Israel exactly as they would another missionary country, and after a few months returned home without results. The situation in Israel is different. First, the people are returning in unbelief. They are bitter toward so-called Christians who have persecuted or killed them through the centuries. Next, they must rebuild the land which is now desert. While they're doing this they have to survive among bitter enemies. They are not in a mood to be confronted with Jesus by someone who reminds them of those who killed their people. Then, finally, it's against the law to have an overt type of witness. The time is not yet for it.

At the conclusion of the performance, the leader of the International Youth Festival at Haifa came forward with his wife and met us. "We are thrilled," they said, "deeply impressed. This is wonderful. What I heard tonight is your spirit and their singing. Without this spirit they would be just another singing group." I did not take this personally because I knew he did not mean it was my spirit, but God's Spirit in me and in the students. I did agree that without God's Spirit our students are no better than any other students who have ability. Then he asked, "Can I have 100 in 1970 at our next International Youth Festival?"

I replied, "You have these 36 coming to sing at your festival next week." He said, "Yes, I am very grateful. But think of what 100 could do. We will be bigger in 1970." I told him we would pray about it.

We prepared to leave for Beersheba and 40 miles on south to the kibbutz of Ben-Gurion. We were to present our program to him at 3 p.m. and then to a large group in the evening. Ben-Gurion has been a modern David. I had a little apprehension, however. Nine years before, he had said to me, "Reverend Roberts, I will not see you again until you learn Hebrew and can speak to me in our language." I had been practicing my limited Hebrew vocabulary for this confrontation. I thought, "What I can't say in words, I will give with God's Spirit in me."

Anxiety had come over me about our visit with Ben-Gurion. Something was wrong and I prayed over it. What I did not know at the time was that our visit with the former prime minister, arranged before we left America, was not known by him. He was not expecting us and did not see people without appointment. Hundreds from America and other lands have failed to see him because of this.

Our guides had known this since morning but were afraid to tell us. We, all 46 of us, were traveling 4 hard hours into the Negev (desert) and 4 hours back, not knowing we had no appointment!

We drove on to the kibbutz in extreme blistering heat. We were all brown then from the Israeli sun anyway, so it didn't matter. We arrived at the appointed hour, 3 p.m. Nobody met us. As we piled out of the vehicles, I noticed all our musical instruments had been left behind. In fact, I suddenly learned our group was unprepared to sing! Something kept gnawing at my stomach. The guides rushed forward to find someone. I said, "Come on, let's follow them."

As we drew near, they were gesticulating with the guards before Ben-Gurion's modest house. The leader knew nothing of our coming and we were not allowed to go farther. The prime minister had received me in 1959. He is the single most important guiding force in the history of modern Israel although now retired and writing his memoirs. There is something about this man our World Action Team needed to see, feel, and carry away with them; and there would be something in them that would be felt by Ben-Gurion and in some inexplicable way by all Israel. The Spirit told me this. I knew it.

Suddenly the leader ducked inside to Ben-Gurion's office. I said to the team, "Start singing."

They said, "What shall we sing?"

"Jerusalem the Gold," I replied.

Inside, Ben-Gurion said, "Who is that singing?"

The guide said, "Oral Roberts from America is here with his students."

Ben-Gurion replied, "Does he have an appointment?" Without waiting for an answer, he said, "Send him in."

I motioned Evelyn to follow and we went in. There he was, older by nine years, his hair still standing straight up on his head, with clear piercing eyes.

"Sit down, sit down," he said.

I recalled our last visit, and Evelyn's conversation with Mrs. Ben-Gurion.

"You knew her?" he asked Evelyn. "That's good." (Mrs. Ben-Gurion had recently died.)

I said, "Mr. Ben-Gurion, our World Action Team, students of Oral Roberts University, are outside waiting to sing for you."

"Good! Let us go to them," he replied.

They were all seated on the grass. Ben-Gurion immediately refused a chair proffered by an aide and sat down with them. The students cheered this and there was instant rapport. I had them sing a song in Hebrew, then "Jerusalem the Gold" again. They continued with "I've Discovered the Way of Gladness," followed by a testimony from Bob Goodwin of our purpose in Israel, the great reception we enjoyed everywhere, and of Christ's love in our hearts.

Ben-Gurion kept saying, "Where did you get such wonderful students?"

As I explained, he said, "They are remarkable."

Handing him my Bible, I asked him to read from it to the students and to speak to them of his feelings about Israel, God, and the world. Taking the Bible he thumbed through it slowly, and abruptly turned to

Genesis. "I'll read only one verse," he said. "So God created man in his own image, in the image of God created he him; male and female created he them." Closing the Bible and laying it on the grass, he looked around at all of us. "The verse reminds us," he said, "that before man was ever a Jew, or Arab, or Christian, he was created a human being. And we must treat each other as human beings."

While we were all deeply moved I asked Ben-Gurion if he would join hands with us for prayer. There in the area where Abraham lived and talked with God, Hebrew and Christian joined hands and spoke to the same God and prayed for all men in every nation.

We all stood up and each shook hands with Ben-Gurion. Turning to me, he said, "I want you to promise to come back."

The students and I said, "God willing, we will return." He smiled, "At least 100 next time."

The next day I flew out to Africa for our crusade there, but I was not disturbed about leaving the World Action Team for two more weeks in Israel. God was with them. He had opened the doors wide and they were anointed by the Holy Spirit to witness. At the International Youth Festival in Haifa, they left an impact upon the youth present from scores of nations as well as upon thousands of Israelis. They were also flown to the Sinai Desert to sing to the soldiers, and again God used them in a remarkable way. An Israeli newspaper reporter who traveled with the ORU students on the special plane provided by the Israeli Air Force could not understand how they could sing and witness as they did. He said, "They're the most exhilarating group that has ever appeared in Israel!"

We still are receiving reports of the impact they had. How we thank God for having had this opportunity to minister among His ancient people.

I'm still under the spell of Israel and I believe that God will continue to use our ministry to witness unto Him "in Jerusalem, and in all Judaea, and in Samaria, and unto the uttermost part of the earth" (Acts 1:8).

We are now standing at a pivotal point in human history. Israel's crucial position in God's timetable warrants our careful scrutiny. Israel is fast becoming a strategic target and temptation to fall prey to the nations that would invade its borders to seek spoil.

Amazing transformations continue in Israel, making it increasingly desirable to enemy nations. Swamplands have become flourishing fields and sand dunes have given place to beautiful orange groves. Millions of crates of citrus fruit are shipped abroad from its new Mediterranean port of Ashdod. Though a young nation, Israel constantly furnishes agricultural, medical, scientific, and educational assistance to lesser-developed nations in Africa, Asia, and Latin America.

There is untold wealth in the Dead Sea and Negev Desert areas. A development program amounting to billions of dollars includes industry, electric power, mining, and housing in southern Negev. Israel's overall economy is growing rapidly. Prosperous modern cities such as Jerusalem, Tel Aviv, and Haifa continue to expand. The Middle East contains immense reserves in oil and chemicals. The coming Antichrist will fully realize the strategic political, economic, and religious position of Israel and will plan accordingly. But what do the Scriptures foretell concerning the successive events which will happen in Israel?

5

Christ's return — Rapture and Revelation

JESUS CHRIST will return to this earth once again, the very One who ascended into the heavens, as testified by 500 witnesses 40 days after His resurrection. There are more than 300 verses in the Bible concerning the Second Coming of Christ, an event as certain to take place in the future as is the fact of His ascension in the past. (Acts 1:11.)

The next event on the calendar of prophecy in God's timetable is the sudden disappearance of a number of persons from all nations of the world — a greater percentage in some, minuscule in others. They will be composed only of those persons who have experienced salvation through a personal confrontation with and faith in Jesus Christ. Although the term is not used in the Bible, this mass exodus of believers from earth is often called the *Rapture*. This event will occur in a moment's time, at the sudden, secret return of Jesus Christ for this select group of human beings.

The signs of the times are to be observed carefully, for they serve as signposts pointing to the Lord's imminent return. It shall be unexpected and unannounced to the world at large. "Watch therefore: for ye know not what hour your Lord doth come" (Matthew 24:42). The next voice calling the Christians may be the voice of the returning Savior. "For the Lord himself shall descend from heaven with a

61

shout . . . and the dead in Christ shall rise first: Then we which are alive and remain shall be caught up together with them in the clouds, to meet the Lord in the air" (1 Thessalonians 4:16, 17). Strange-sounding words? So were the first human sounds coming to earth from the lunar orbit a quarter of a million miles away in outer space that Christmas in 1968. If mortal man was able to produce such a staggering feat, why should people doubt the Scriptures and the power of Almighty God?

Believers in Christ who have died shall be raised simultaneously from all the graveyards of past time. The believers on earth shall instantly join them in the flight to keep Christ's appointment in outer space. From this rendezvous Christ shall escort this noble company of regenerated individuals to heaven. There, all the translated ones shall appear for the believer's rewards, called the Judgment Seat of Christ. Upon the basis of each believer's work accomplished on earth following his conversion experience, the rewards shall be announced. "For we must all appear before the judgment seat of Christ; that every one may receive the things done in his body, according to that he hath done, whether it be good or bad" (2 Corinthians 5:10). This judgment is not to be confused with the Great White Throne Judgment destined for unbelievers and separated from the former by a millenium. Following the judgment in heaven, the risen redeemed, also described as the Bride of Christ, shall partake of the marvelous Marriage Supper with Jesus Christ. (Revelation 19:7-9.)

But what about the Great Tribulation? Are not the believers to taste of this bitter cup before they experience the glory of translation? Will Christ return for them before, during, or after this Tribulation?

There are many who teach that true believers will experience at least a part, if not all, of the Great Tribulation. Do the Scriptures shed any light upon the chronology of these end-time events? What will be the relationship of the Second Coming of Christ to the Great Tribulation? Luke 21:36 alerts all believers in this manner, "Watch ye therefore, and pray always, that ye may be accounted worthy to escape all these things that shall come to pass, and to stand before the Son of man." Notice the word escape.

Before the awful storm of the Tribulation, terrors shall break upon the earth. Those who are living for Christ and are looking for His appearance (Hebrews 9:28) shall be translated, suddenly caught away to meet the Lord in the air. They shall be safely above earth's storm. This does not mean that God's faithful will never experience trials or bitter persecutions. At this moment in various parts of the world, severe persecution, imprisonment, and even torture are plaguing those who refuse to deny their Lord. I have not been a stranger to persecution for the cause of Jesus Christ, and I know many others who suffer also. But the Bible indicates that the redeemed Bride of Christ will escape from the unspeakable terrors of the Tribulation, by means of the Rapture. Notice these verses in Revelation 3:10 and 11, "Because thou hast kept the word of my patience, I also will keep thee from the hour of temptation, which shall come upon all the world, to try them that dwell upon the earth. Behold, I come quickly: hold that fast which thou hast, that no man take thy crown."

In the two phases of Jesus' coming the secretive Rapture will precede the public revelation. In the Rapture, Christ appears momentarily for the great meeting in space. At that time He will not descend to earth, nor will He be seen by any not included in the translation. His revelation, however, shall bring the Great Tribulation to a close in the Battle of Armageddon. The diabolical forces of evil will be destroyed by the brightness of His glory and the millenial reign of righteousness will be ushered in by Jesus Christ.

Many people are frightened when the coming of Christ is mentioned. They are either misinformed about this vital subject or there is something wrong with their spiritual experience and relationship. They generally confuse the events that shall occur at the revelation with those that occur at the Rapture. Understand that Christ cannot come *with* the redeemed host until He first comes *for* this company of believers. One event naturally precedes the other.

Further light is gained from 2 Thessalonians 2:7, 8. "For the mystery of iniquity doth already work [the trend toward accepting Antichrist]: only he who now letteth [restrains] will let, until he be taken out of the way. And then [when the Holy Spirit who restrains and convicts mankind of sin be taken] shall that Wicked [the Antichrist] be revealed." In other words, the power of the Holy Spirit in restraining the forces of sin and evil in this world is mightier than the power of Satan. God's power is present in the world, curbing limitless lawlessness and hindering the public clamor for the Antichrist. No earthly power is greater than the power of Satan, for as the prince of the power of the air, he controls principalities, powers, and rulers. (Ephesians 2:2; 6:12.) Only the power of the Holy Spirit supersedes the power of the enemy of men's souls, minds, and bodies. The Church Invisible is made up of individuals the world around who are indwelt by the Holy Spirit, and the Word declares, "Greater is he that is in you, than he that is in the world" (1 John 4:4). When the convicting power of the Holy Spirit is removed, then each Christian shall also be taken out of the way. This will enable the forces of evil to abound as never before. Today's active presence of the Holy Spirit through the consecrated lives of redeemed men and women is circumscribing lawlessness and godlessness within certain bounds, as a great dam or seawall holds back the turbulent waters.

The Holy Spirit will not and cannot absent himself from the earthly scene without also removing the believers. He will not desert God's faithful, leaving them to the holocaust of the Great Tribulation. No, they have an appointment with Jesus Christ in the Rapture.

Since the Holy Spirit is coequal with the Father and the Son, and coeternal, He is also omnipresent. The distinct difference in the ministry of the Holy Spirit in post-Rapture days and during the Tribulation is that He will no longer actively minister as the restrainer of the Antichrist spirit. Despite His withdrawal, however, the omnipresent Spirit will yet enable some men to refuse the demands of Antichrist, even to the point of martyrdom. The Scriptures reveal that people will exercise faith for salvation during the agonizing years of the Great Tribulation. John makes mention of them in Revelation 7:9-17, saying, "What are these which are arrayed in white robes? and whence came they? . . . These are they which came out of great tribulation, and have washed their robes, and made them white in the blood of the Lamb. . . . and God shall wipe away all tears from their eyes."

The criterion for becoming a candidate for the Rapture is to know the One who will initiate the event. Any person may be reconciled to God through the meritorious work of Jesus Christ on the Cross of Calvary by inviting Christ to become one's personal Savior. Turning from his human way his eye is on Jesus, the Author and Perfector of his faith. Growing daily in the grace and knowledge of his Lord and Savior, the new believer is a candidate for the Rapture, added to that great number to be caught up in an Elijahlike translation experience when Christ returns for His own. No person on earth knows the day nor the hour of Christ's Second Coming since the divine design is to encourage believers to look for that blessed hope, the imminent return of the Lord. (Matthew 24:36-44.)

The signs of the time, God's timetable of prophecies, indicate the possibility of the near coming of Christ. Meanwhile "We ourselves groan within ourselves, waiting for the adoption, to wit, the redemption of our body. For we are saved by hope: but hope that is seen is not hope: for what a man seeth, why doth he yet hope for it? But if we hope for that we see not, then do we with patience wait for it" (Romans 8:23-25.)

From Adam's day to this, believers shall "be changed, in a moment, in the twinkling of an eye, at the last trump: for the trumpet shall sound, and the dead shall be raised incorruptible. Then we which are alive and remain shall be caught up together with them in the clouds, to meet the Lord in the air: (1 Corinthians 15:52; 1 Thessalonians 4:17). What a space trip!

The rapid release of underground missiles and the underseas Polaris missiles are not to be compared with the instantaneous resurrection of the dead in Christ from graves in earth and sea. The fantastic speed of the astronauts' lunar capsules will seem motionless as millions of believers rush past at a speed greater than light to keep their appointment with the Lord Jesus Christ in outer space!

When one belongs to Christ, how comforting is the concept of the soon return of the Lord. Apostle Paul wrote "Wherefore, comfort one another with these words" (1 Thessalonians 4:18). The early Christians greeted each other by saying, "Maranatha," which means the Lord cometh. They were encouraged and cheered despite the persecution confronting them on every hand. The thrones of royalty and power-maddened potentates were unable to dim their vision of the majesty of their coming King of kings. For long centuries down the corridor of time the Church Invisible has waited for the Rapture. Here is wisdom. Believers should occupy until He comes (Luke 19:13), by planning a life that will count for eternity as well as time. Hold lightly the material blessings which may come your way in an affluent society. Use your talents redemptively by being an effective witness, turning the attention of those who cross your pathway to Christ and His relevance to the needs of today's world. Maranatha!

But what about those who are left behind, the vast majority of the world's population who are not launched into outer space for that celestial rendezvous with Christ?

6

Antichrist shall come

FROM THE APOCALYPTIC BOOKS of Daniel and Revelation we gain a perspective, a mountaintop view of events which will occur during the Great Tribulation. Interpretations vary, but this is no reason to abandon a long, hard look at God's forecast of the future.

Evil men and evil deeds are increasing in our troubled society, threatening to engulf the entire human family. But post-Rapture days will usher in sin as a tidal wave, arising to its climactic height to wash away the vestiges of righteousness.

The world stage will be set for the introduction of the Antichrist, also named the man of sin, son of perdition, and the Beast in the Scriptures. (2 Thessalonians 2:3; Revelation 13: 1, 3; 1 John 2:18.) The mastermind behind the scenes, the one who will introduce the Antichrist, is Satan, who is also called the devil, the accuser of the brethren, the dragon, the old serpent, etc., in the Bible. I am fully aware of the tendency today to reject the biblical teaching concerning the existence and machinations of a personal being called Satan. But I believe the Word of God and its treatment of Satan as a being possessing great power which he uses to unleash negative forces in the lives of men and nations.

Who is Satan? Did God create the devil? No. There was a time when no devil existed. Rather, a being was created after the angelic order of beings, one appointed to a position of high authority, one of the most exalted of God's angels. This aspect of his past is revealed in Ezekiel 28:12-19, a passage dealing with but going beyond the king of Tyrus. Many artists characterize the devil with hoofs, horns and a tail. No such description of him may be found in the Bible. Originally, he was the perfect example of all that was beautiful in God's creation. It was his great beauty and brightness that occasioned his fall. His heart was lifted up and pride began to corrupt his wisdom. Iniquity was found in him and for the first time in the history of God's great universe there was a discordant note.

Another passage of Scripture reveals his original name as Lucifer, son of the morning, (Isaiah 14:12-15) in a context also referring to the king of Babylon. God pronounced judgment on Lucifer when his egotism became so distorted that he believed himself to be co-equal to God. And in the fall of Lucifer we have the story of the origin of Satan. For when Lucifer's swollen pride caused him to believe in his heart that his justifiable goal was to be exalted like the Most High, he had reached the point of no return. In his deposition to the prince of this world, Satan is dedicated to destroying all traces of God from the world. For thousands of years he has continued his diabolical work as the arch-enemy of God. Apostle Paul recognized him as "the prince of the power of the air" (Ephesians 2:2). Evicted from God's presence in heaven, Satan designed the downfall of the human race which had been created in the image of God.

Now Satan's time is limited and we may expect the escalation of his end-time plan to destroy mankind. "Woe to the inhabiters of the earth and of the sea! for the devil is come down unto you, having great wrath, because he knoweth that he hath but a short time" (Revelation 12:12).

And this leads us to discover what the role of the Antichrist will be in relation to the Great Tribulation. Behind the scenes Satan will commandeer and administer his master plan to rule the world in totalitarian domination. Great will be his wrath, brief his time, and feverish his activities. The wicked plans and programs he has employed in the past will be superseded as he proceeds to blot the name of God out of men's lives and prepares the way of Antichrist. Satan is a spirit-being and can only operate in the world through the minds and wills of men, through human instrumentalities. Clandestinely, he will prepare minds for the full acceptance of the Antichrist. Although his hope for ultimate victory is vain, Satan will attempt to destroy men for time and eternity.

"Antichrist shall come" (1 John 2:18) is the inspired announcement. Satan will propose to this unique person, alive at this critical time, an unusual offer. Only once before was such an offer made by Satan, and this to the Lord Jesus Christ. The account of that confrontation states that "the devil taketh him up into an exceeding high mountain, and sheweth him all the kingdoms of the world, and the glory of them; And saith unto him, All these things will I give thee, if thou wilt fall down and worship me. Then saith Jesus unto him, Get thee hence, Satan: for it is written, Thou shalt worship the Lord thy God, and him only shalt thou serve. Then the devil leaveth him . . . " (Matthew 4:8-11).

This important passage throws much light on the

method Satan may employ in producing the Antichrist. In tempting Christ, Satan was prepared to grant Him the kingdoms of this world and in return Christ was to be subservient to the tempter. Jesus rejected the offer and Satan retreated. A similar temptation shall reoccur in the Tribulation and the devil shall be rewarded with success. Shown the glittering glory of this world, Antichrist shall accept the conditions in order to be the recipient of almost unlimited power. Men of renown will seek him and rulers of the earth shall agree to become his subservients.

Antichrist will appear to be a whole man from the naturalistic point of view. He will be the embodiment of the naturalistic philosophies and religions — those which have denied the Bible, the deity and vicarious atonement of Jesus Christ. With Antichrist's winsome personality, majestic bearing, and extraordinary intellect, the world will little realize the true identity of this person. He must do the will of Satan, submitting his mind, soul, and body to his god. In complete conspiracy with the devil, the Antichrist will receive Satanic power and authority. (Revelation 13:2.) From that hour Satan will lavish his powers upon the man who has entered into a covenant with him, the man who shall shortly usurp the power attributed to God and be recognized eventually as the Antichrist of prophecy.

In a relatively short span of time his business acumen and political skill will be recognized, causing him to be catapulted to fame and prestige. His name will be included in the daily conversation of millions around the world. His counsel will be eagerly sought by those shouldering immense national burdens. International telecasts will project him before national leaders who will become increasingly impressed by his uncommon abilities. World figures will seek his counsel and wisdom as did the Queen of Sheba when she sought out King Solomon.

With the redeemed people gone from the earth, and the removal of the restraining power of the Holy Spirit, Satan will be operating behind the scenes of human men with virtually unbridled power. Respect for law and order still existing will begin to disappear. Without the Holy Spirit who convicts of sin and guides into all truth, the Antichrist will have every opportunity to delude the world. Men will fall victims to Satan's plans to glorify the Antichrist, drawn by an unseen force to lavish praise on the intriguing, fascinating Antichrist.

Under insurmountable problems, heads of nations will become desperate. Mounting distress and perplexity will increase in the area of international economics. Endlessly drawn-out cold-war economics will sap the strength of the strongest nations. Deficit spending will pass the peak danger points. Overwhelming national debts will destroy public confidence in national monetary units.

International monetary exchanges will continue to funnel huge amounts of money to the underdeveloped emerging nations. However, due to their exploding populations, these weaker nations will outgrow their food-production capacities and remain in relative poverty.

Excessive spending for economic and military aid around the world will have taken its perilous toll. Foreign-held claims on the gold balances could cause the wealthier nations to collapse financially. In panic, citizens will surrender their rights to leaders who present pragmatic solutions. Fear of chaos will be so great that they will entrust these national leaders with dictatorial powers.

Insoluble world conditions will increase in complexity. The resources of the nations shall be exhausted and ominous depressions will threaten to spread rapidly. The common-market philosophy will spread and new alliances will be formed. Peace treaties will be signed and attempts to destroy nuclear stockpiles will be made.

From such situations nations shall tend to pool their resources and form an amalgamated empire. Ten nations will unite in a federation in an effort to survive. However, new problems will be created, demanding unusually gifted leadership. Frustrated by failures, facing bankruptcy and political disaster, there will be a cry for a "superman."

The rulers will recognize Antichrist's superhuman organizational abilities and his extraordinary power to accomplish seemingly impossible tasks. The rulers of the 10 nations will accept the proposal to hold a major conference with this great personage. Why had they not considered this meeting sooner? This conference will be destined to change the course of the world.

The situation will cause Satan to advance his master plan. Before the important conference is to convene, a private meeting with two chief participants will be held. Satan and Antichrist will set forth intricate plans in preparation for the summit meeting with 10 of the great rulers of the world. Finally, Satan's details will be worked out with Antichrist, the messianic counterfeit.

At the summit meeting the 10 kings will be delighted to discover that Antichrist possesses a detailed program that contains all the requisites of success. It is the work of a genius and is thus recognized by the 10 kings who then arrive at a major decision. "And the ten horns which thou sawest are ten kings, . . . These have one mind, and shall give their power and strength unto the beast" (Revelation 17:12, 13).

We do not know the program Antichrist will initiate but it will be successful in revolutionizing industry, agriculture and commerce. Energized by Satan, Antichrist will bring widespread prosperity to the world. Under his skillful administration, technology will keep abreast with the expanding needs of the day. Despite increased automation, new employment opportunities will be created. Agriculture shall flourish. Poverty shall be erased, want and squalor eliminated, and civil order will be restored. He will be heralded as a world savior, the champion of human interests. Without equal, his brilliant accomplishments will captivate mankind, causing men to pledge allegiance to Antichrist.

There are many who are looking for a vicious beast-like ruler to be the Antichrist, but he will never appear in this manner. He will be too cunning, too adroit. However, in the closing 3½ years of his reign his true nature shall be exposed, from a friend to the downtrodden and champion of world peace (Daniel 8:25), to the covenant breaker, the Antichrist (Daniel 9:27).

His early acceptance by the masses will be predicated upon his wondrous ability to bring order out of chaos and success out of defeat. The world will never willingly seek a ruler who exhibits ferocious, beastlike qualities. His true identity will be subtly camouflaged by Satan.

During World War II many religious writers prophesied that Adolph Hitler was the Antichrist. But he came as a man of war and terror, a mad beast determined to destroy free society, defeat the democracies, exterminate the Jews, and dominate the entire world for a millennium. One of his first acts after coming to power was to initiate a reign of terror against the Jews. His war machine overran countries whose only desire was to remain at peace with neighbor nations. Nearly all of Europe fell helplessly before his massive blitzkrieg. Consequently, he became the world's most hated and feared man. True allegiance cannot be permanently gained by threat and intimidation. When Hitler singled out the Jews as the primary target of his bestial reign of terror he introduced his own doom, for he that curses God's ancient people Israel shall be cursed.

But Antichrist, before his exposure during the last 42 months of terrible tribulation, shall be riding the wave of world popularity, prestige and power. He will not be content with the rulership of the 10 kingdoms that sought his aid. This will serve as a steppingstone to world domination. From rulership over an amalgamated empire, Antichrist will expand by means of military conquests and a war of nerves until he successfully outmaneuvers all nations and becomes the world dictator. "And power was given him over all kindreds, and tongues and nations" (Revelation 13:7). The flag of Antichrist will fly over each and every capital of the world, including the United States of America.

Antichrist will introduce a unilateral rearmament program in which all nations will agree to disarm, with the exception of his military forces which will control the world, ostensibly for peaceful purposes. According to Revelation 9:16, it appears that some 200 million soldiers will be in preparation for the war to end all wars, the Battle of Armageddon. While crusading for world peace, the Antichrist will actually be positioning the world's largest army for the struggle to death against the King of kings and His army of the redeemed.

The spirit of the Antichrist is already in the world. "And this is that spirit of antichrist, whereof ye have heard that it should come; and even now is it in the world" (1 John 4:3). The spirit of Antichrist is eternally and unalterably opposed to Jesus Christ. This spirit is spreading throughout the world, inducing men and women to hate righteousness, to hate God or to deny His existence. This willful rejection of truth and goodness will prepare men for the deception of Antichrist, the Great Tribulation, the Battle of Armageddon, and eternal destruction.

7

Satan's triad and the great Tribulation

THE 42 MONTHS of Tribulation shall be a period of unparalleled suffering involving all nations of the earth, and especially Israel. It is the last half of Daniel's 70th week which will follow the dispensation of the Gospel Age. This prophetical week consists of seven years following the rapture of the redeemed from the earth. The nations will be bereft of the presence, power, prayers, and wholesome activities of its most righteous inhabitants. The restraining influence of the Holy Spirit will be lifted, the salt of the earth removed, leaving men to satiate their most evil appetites and demonic drives. Imagine living in a city in which God had removed His redeemed people.

This reminds me of my visit to Moscow. It was the day before Easter Sunday and I had visited the Kremlin. I also entered the mausoleum in which the dead bodies of both Lenin and Stalin were displayed before the latter was removed as a result of Russia's de-Stalinization program. I thought of the years of purposeful design in which these men were engaged in stripping the minds of the Russian children and youth of their belief in God. I had yet to meet a single person who admitted his belief in God. I thought to myself, "I've not attended church yet. I feel as though I'm surrounded with unbelief and it's my first time to be in a country so wholly without God. How strong are the demon powers here. How restless, tense and depressed it makes one feel."

At the American Embassy in Moscow the following impressions were shared with me:

"Russia has no place for God in her plans. She is looking to herself and herself alone. She does not ask for people to pray, to read the Bible, to call on God, or to keep spiritual perspective. It is her way to power that she is depending on. Through this she is controlling her people, making them work, bringing prosperity and goods to the world market. She is pushing her scientists to bring forth new weapons to destroy those who do not agree with her. She muzzles her churches and teaches her youth that God is a myth and Christianity is a legend. She says that in a few years, after the old die off, her youth will make Russia a country completely without God. It will be a Communist paradise in which God has no part."

In far greater measure the Tribulation will encompass a time when God is ignored, despised, and blasphemed by the world at large. Sin will break out in epidemic proportions, and wickedness will be evidenced as never before. Lawlessness shall abound as Satan is permitted greater license and will exercise almost limitless power in the lives of men. He will be obsessed with a burning desire to eradicate all memories of Christianity and to blot God's name from the earth. It will be a time when the abyss is opened and demons are permitted to torment men upon the earth, a time when the extreme wickedness and degeneracy of mankind and their delight in such sin will cause God to leave them to their own extremities. (2 Thessalonians 2.)

Revelation 13 reveals the completion of Satan's unholy triad by introducing the False Prophet. Martin Luther once remarked that the devil was the "ape of God." The counterfeit trinity will be composed of Satan, Antichrist, and the False Prophet. Satan, ever attempting to usurp God's authority, will cause great wonders to be displayed before mankind through Antichrist and the False Prophet.

Realizing the strategic, political, economic, and religious position of Israel, Antichrist will be most careful to win the confidence of the Jewish people, inspire their homage and convince them that he is their Messiah. Daniel 9:27 reveals the fact that he will make a covenant with them at the beginning of the seven years of his reign. This alliance is one in which Israel makes "a covenant with death, and with hell are we at agreement" (Isaiah 28:15). Jesus said, "I am come in my Father's name, and ye receive me not: if another come in his own name, him ye will receive" (John 5:43). Why did not the Jews accept Jesus as their Messiah? Jesus came in an entirely different manner from that in which He was expected. The Jews were expecting the "Lion" out of the tribe of Judah, and Jesus came as a "Bleeding Lamb," slain from the foundation of the world; they looked for a financial wizard, but at one time Jesus sent Peter to fish to pay His taxes; they dreamed of a conqueror that would break the iron rule of Rome and exalt them to high positions, but Jesus cried, "My kingdom is not of this world"; and finally allowed a Roman procurator to sentence Him to a shameful death at Calvary. But Antichrist will meet the Jews' expectations. He shall recognize their national aspirations, give them greater prestige, allow them special privileges, and more firmly establish them in Israel. If the temple is not already built, he will aid them in its erection, restore its worship, and allow them to offer daily sacrifices. Thus, at his inception of rulership, representatives of Israel will go to the council room of the Antichrist. They will agree to sign a covenant for seven years. (Daniel 9:27.)

Midway through the covenant, Revelation 13:3 and 4 suggest that Antichrist will be assassinated. "And I saw one of his heads as it were wounded to death; and his deadly wound was healed . . . the beast which had the wound by a sword, and did live." It is important to note that Antichrist is also called "that man of sin, the son of perdition" (2 Thessalonians 2:3) and he is spoken of as "the beast that . . . was, and is not; and shall ascend out of the bottomless pit, and go into perdition" (Revelation 17:8). Suggested here is the possibility of a twofold wonder perpetrated by Satan in the resurrection of Antichrist and the assignment of a demonic spirit from the abyss to take the seat of authority in this man of sin.

Upon the healing of his deadly wound, the world will wonder after Antichrist and will worship him saying, "Who is like unto the beast? who is able to make war with him? And there was given unto him a mouth speaking great things and blasphemies; and power was given unto him to continue forty and two months" (Revelation 13:4, 5).

Worshiped by the masses and endowed with tremendous power, Antichrist will endeavor to conquer the very souls of men. To aid in this unholy ambition the third member of the triad of Satan will appear — the False Prophet. While Antichrist has majored in the military, political, commercial, industrial, and agricultural aspects of men's lives, the False Prophet will be introduced as a religious leader, an idealistic holy man. He will apparently desire the betterment of the world, but will shortly prove to be a wolf in sheep's clothing.

A true prophet receives his call and inspiration to preach the gospel from above, but the False Prophet will obtain his call, inspiration, and power from below. He will be the consummation of all past and present false preachers, prophets, and religious leaders. The powers of deception will be increased a thousandfold as the False Prophet effectively deludes the whole world with his false doctrine.

Satan will introduce the False Prophet as his representative of religion into the world to capture and control the spiritual aspirations of humanity. Knowing that religious allegiance is stronger than political support, Satan will combine the powers of the False Prophet and Antichrist to fulfill his design against any traces of Christianity.

The most deep-seated part of man's nature is that desire to worship someone or something. This religious drive is the strongest faculty in his life. Russia has experienced more than half a century of atheistic rulership, during which time there have been four massive antireligious purges in which many clergymen were imprisoned, exiled in slave labor camps, or killed. In Communist classrooms the existence of God is denied. Soviet books, periodicals, films, and plays are designed to discredit all faiths and lead to complete atheism. Yet, despite all these programs, religious belief prevails. Why? Because the spiritual aspect of man's life is constantly crying for expression.

America is greatly indebted to the spiritual impetus provided by the pioneering of its pilgrim forefathers. Their desire to worship God with complete freedom of conscience was so intense that they willingly left their homeland and crossed the briny deep to find a new world in which they could freely exercise their religious beliefs. This ever-present desire to worship God gave them power, strength, and courage to face the dangers and hardships of the new world. And whoever rules men spiritually, truly rules their lives. The Antichrist will realize that he can best succeed as an earthly ruler when he grants his subjects an outlet for their spiritual inclinations. Unless he offers a world religion, his reign may be brief. This is precisely where the third actor of the drama of the end time will be spotlighted. He will appear as an angel of light to lead men into a new religion which will be hailed and honored. To initiate his campaign for a new world religious order and system he will inspire the world to worship Antichrist, presenting a religious basis for people's whole-hearted worship of Satan's substitute. Because they loved not the truth, they will be completely receptive to the delusion. The False Prophet shall discredit the Scriptures and Christ by exalting the Antichrist as the only one living on earth who has been assassinated by the sword, yet risen from the dead. Further supportive evidence will be submitted when an image of Antichrist is erected and subsequently given life and speech! (Revelation 13:15.) The False Prophet will determinedly glorify and deify the Antichrist in order to inspire and coerce the world to pay him supreme homage.

"And he exerciseth all the power of the first beast

before him" (Revelation 13:12). Antichrist, the first beast, maintained authority over all kindred, tongues, and nations as their political dictator. The False Prophet shall be given the same degree of power over man's religious life and so function as man's religious ruler. The world's people will come to realize that their lives are overshadowed and ruled politically by Antichrist and spiritually by the False Prophet, the evil emissaries of Satan.

As a result of this totalitarian power religious freedom will disappear from the world. Existing religious establishments will be forced to worship Antichrist. The Holy Bible and other religious books will be banned, declared irrelevant, and worse, harmful. The False Prophet shall publish a new bible, presenting Antichrist as God. It may even contain gospels recording the miracles and wonders of Antichrist. Its laws will be issued by Satan and the people will be commanded to worship the unholy trinity. "And they worshipped the dragon which gave power unto the beast: and they worshipped the beast, saying, Who is like unto the beast?" (Revelation 13:4).

Forerunners of the religion of Antichrist are already in the world today. Scores of religions deny that Jesus Christ is the Son of God and in a sense are preparing the way for the Tribulation religion that shall ascribe its worship to Antichrist. All opposition shall be crushed by the new dictatorial government of Antichrist. Remaining clergymen and religious leaders will be obliged to exalt the Antichrist as God or be summarily executed. Special training will prepare puppet ministers to preach Antichrist and his new religion. This is not difficult for us to conceive. In Red China, noncooperative pastors have been subjected to brainwashing, torture, and ignominious deaths.

This present world order has repeatedly rejected Christ. Worship days are ignored, God's laws are despised, and men are lovers of pleasures more than lovers of God, having a form of godliness, but denying its power. Yes, the world will accept Antichrist!

The False Prophet shall deceive the world by means of miracles which he shall have power to perform in that day. Yes, he will be a miracle worker. Miracles have always been the evidence of a person's religious power. By this means faith is begotten in human hearts. When Christ was upon the earth, He proved himself to be God's only begotten Son by mighty miracles. Jesus broke up funeral processions, robbed the grave of its victims, walked across the windswept, storm-tossed Sea of Galilee, healed the sick and afflicted, opened blinded eyes, unstopped deaf ears, made the dumb to sing, and the crippled to walk. By these great miracles many people accepted Him as the Son of the living God and became new creations in Christ. But with Satanic power, the False Prophet shall perform miracles, not in order to lift men out of sin into abundant living, but rather to enslave, debase and destroy them. All the power of the devil will be at his command.

He will be empowered to call down fire from the skies. Possibly this will take place in one of the world's largest cities. Thousands will be assembled under a cloudless sky and a brilliant sun. Suddenly, with outstretched hands "he maketh fire come down from heaven on the earth in the sight of men, And deceiveth them that dwell on the earth by the means of those miracles which he had power to do in the sight of the beast; saying to them that dwell on the earth, that they should make an image to the beast, which had the wound by a sword, and did live" (Revelation 13:13, 14).

We have seen its type in the colossal image that King Nebuchadnezzar had erected in the plain of Dura (Daniel 3:1-6); where people fell down and worshiped the golden image. In all probability Antichrist's image will be erected in Jerusalem. At the dedication of this unusual image, telecasters, radio announcers, newsmen, many officials and dignitaries will be among the thousands gathered from all parts of the world. Millions at home will view the proceedings via telstar or listen to the event via shortwave radios. Antichrist will be present, surrounded by his illustrious celebrities. The main speaker for the auspicious occasion will be none other than the False Prophet. He is there to dedicate the image to the world's greatest humanitarian, the Antichrist. During his laudatory speech he stretches forth his hand and touches the image. Suddenly, to the amazement of all, he commands the image to speak. Never before has life been produced from an inanimate image. Scientists have tried and failed. Only life begets life.

Soviet scientists have long been engaged in research projects to bring the deceased back to life without causing irreparable brain damage. There have been successes with human beings during the interval categorized as clinical death, that is, those who have been medically dead but a few minutes. But any totalitarian power would be ecstatic if it could infuse life into an inanimate image. As the cities around the world view this event and the multitude looks on with breathless suspense, the image comes to life and begins to speak. A miracle of miracles! Never before has anything of this nature happened in the history of the world. At the command of the False Prophet he causes "that as many as would not worship the image of the beast should be killed" (Revelation 13:15).

It is my belief that this image shall be placed in the temple in Jerusalem, rebuilt by this time. Within the temple's holy place this image will represent an absolute desecration of Israel's worship to Jehovah. This is the abomination of desolation spoken of by Jesus in Matthew 24:15-22. When the Jews see the image in the temple, standing in the holy place, their eyes shall be opened to the delusions and deceit of the False Prophet and Antichrist. They shall unequivocally refuse to bow to the image, for deeply imbedded in their religious beliefs is the abhorrence of all idolatry, especially bowing to any image. A large number of Gentiles shall be made aware of the deception and will also refuse to bow. This bold defiance shall spread rapidly, causing many to reject the Antichrist. Multitudes shall perceive the great deception and turn in full obedience to the true God and Jesus Christ. In so doing, Jew and Gentile alike shall incur the wrath of the Antichrist, who shall spew out a reign of terror that has one minor parallel in biblical history.

Centuries ago the three Hebrew children had a choice, either to bow to Nebuchadnezzar's image of gold, or burn in his fiery furnace, essentially the same basic decision which will face the contemporaries of the dreaded Antichrist. There are two laws which men live by — the law of faith and the law of compromise. Compromise is held up as the standard to live by in this 20th century. One will either bow or he will burn. But if one compromises the Word, the truth and life in Christ, he will untimately lose what he may gain by compromise.

The three Hebrew children proved their total commitment to God when they confronted the dictator and said, "O Nebuchadnezzar, we are not careful to answer thee in this matter. If it be so, our God whom we serve is able to deliver us from the burning fiery furnace, and he will deliver us out of thine hand, O King" (Daniel 3:16, 17). He is able. In essence, they declared that "God is able. But if He doesn't see fit to do it, we may burn in your furnace, but we will not bow to your god."

In the Great Tribulation, Antichrist will blaspheme the name of God and issue the command that all who refuse to bow to his image must die. Those who with conviction and courage turn from the idolatrous image of Antichrist to receive Christ and keep the commandments of God will have the option of recanting or face immediate execution. All the power of Satan will be released against those who yet fear God. Their lives shall be in jeopardy every moment. Those who were left behind at the Rapture, the professing but nonpossessing Christians, will face a martyr's route to heaven if they stand up for Jesus Christ. Many will flee into the mountains, dens and caves of the earth, none will remain alive without recanting and worshiping the Antichrist.

How will this be perpetrated? During the last 3½ years, the False Prophet, the third member of the unholy triad, "causeth all, both small and great, rich and poor, free and bond, to receive a mark in their right hand, or in their foreheads" (Revelation 13:16). This will be a universally recognized mark.

Fully necessary as the medium of exchange will be this mark, or the name of Antichrist, or his number, 666. (Revelation 13:17, 18).

The mark will be very beautiful, devised by the cunning mind of Antichrist to symbolize and secure the complete allegiance, obedience, and worship of the people. The mark, name, or number, will irreversibly unite the world to himself. As the terrible toll exacted from the world for being its problem solver, Antichrist and the False Prophet will force the acceptance of mark, name, or number as proof of everyone's absolute subjection to the unholy triad. Lacking complete identification with Antichrist, men will be unable to survive, for they will be positively prohibited from buying and selling.

Visualize the awesome developments during this totalitarian reign of Antichrist. Shoppers at supermarkets will be obliged to exhibit the Beast's identification at each checkout counter or else leave without being able to purchase food. Those who persist in refusing to be identified as Satan's property will face rejection on every hand. Where may they go? Leave the neighborhood, county, state, or country? Not without the ability to purchase gasoline or transportation tickets by land, sea or air. There will be no escape. The same condition shall prevail throughout the earth. An elaborate and thorough espionage system will make evasion virtually impossible. In that day even brother will turn against brother and father against son. There will be absolutely no buying or selling without the mark, name, or number of the Beast.

The farmer will have his produce confiscated unless he identifies with Antichrist. Manufacturers will try to discover a neutral market for the sales of their merchandise, but exchange will be impossible without the Satanic identification.

The fires of the Great Tribulation will break upon the Jews with intense fury. Neither man nor woman will be spared. Upon refusal to worship the Antichrist, they shall be slaughtered like sheep with the exception of those fortunate enough to escape to the mountain fastnesses. In anticipation of that terrible "time of Jacob's trouble," Jesus said, "Then let them which be in Judaea flee into the mountains: Let him which is on the housetop not come down to take anything out of his house: Neither let him which is in the field return back to take his clothes" (Matthew 24:16-18). Leaving properties and possessions behind, they will be fortunate indeed to flee for their lives. South of Jerusalem, in the region of Petra, are places where one could probably be hidden indefinitely.

A Jewish leader who has been through this Petra district many times, informed me that its safeholds were impenetrable and one could defy discovery without fear of arrest. The Arabs have hidden there, carrying on their terrorism against the pioneering Jews. In these caves shall many of the fleeing Jews find refuge from Antichrist's dragnet.

God has already prepared a surprise for these fugitives. Before his death at the age of 94, William E. Blackstone had a revelation from God that many of the fleeing Jews, awakened to their awful betrayal at the hands of Antichrist, would find refuge in the dens and caves of the mountain fastnesses around Petra. From a $5-million trust fund Dr. Blackstone dispatched a corps of Christian workers to Petra more than a decade before Israel became a nation in 1948. They transported great cases of Hebrew Bibles, encased in copper boxes. They were sealed in hewn-out vaults in the mountainside of the Petra region against the day when, according to the Bible, the Jews will flee from Jerusalem to the Petra Mountain. In the midst of the Great Tribulation, these Bibles with marked passages will be found, tracing the lineage of Christ, and the working and deceit of Antichrist will be exposed to the persecuted Israelis. These marked passages will show the Jewish people how they have been deceived, betrayed by the Antichrist, and that Jesus Christ is truly their Messiah, their only hope. Only the future will reveal the results of this unique venture of Dr. Blackstone. Undoubtedly God is mysteriously working, even now, for the opportune moment when His Word will be a direct medium in opening the eyes of His ancient people who have been in spiritual blindness so long. That is another reason why we have distributed more than 100,000 Hebrew Bibles in the Holy Land.

Driven, humiliated, persecuted, the Jewish people at last shall realize that true peace and real security are to be found only in the Holy One of Israel, who "came unto his own and his own received him not." God will raise up leaders among them, especially the two witnesses (Revelation 11:3-12) who will, as true prophets, have the testimony of Jesus. (Revelation 19:10.) In the caves and dens of the earth the Jewish people will realize that they have rejected their own beloved Messiah. "And I will pour upon the house of David, and upon the inhabitants of Jerusalem, the spirit of grace and of supplications: and they shall look upon me whom they have pierced, and they shall mourn for him, as . . . for his only son" (Zechariah 12:10).

Thus, despite impossible circumstances, many thousands will refuse to receive the mark of Antichrist. Instead, they will receive Jesus Christ as Lord of their future and love not their lives unto death. Far worse than financial ruin, physical deprivation, starvation, or even martyrdom, will be the judgment awaiting those who do accept the mark of the Beast. "If any man worship the beast and his image, and receive his mark in his forehead, or in his hand, The same shall drink of the wine of the wrath of God, which is poured out without mixture into the cup of his indignation; and he shall be tormented with fire and brimstone in the presence of the holy angels, and in the presence of the Lamb: And the smoke of their torment ascendeth up for ever and ever: and they have no rest day nor night, who worship the beast and his image, and whosoever receiveth the mark of his name. Here is the patience of the saints: here are they that keep the commandments of God, and the faith of Jesus. And I heard a voice from heaven saying . . . Blessed are the dead which die in the Lord" (Revelation 14:9-13).

In the midst of Tribulation horrors the Jews shall mourn for the Messiah. "Alas! for that day is great, so that none is like it, it is even the time of Jacob's trouble, but he shall be saved out of it." God shall hear their cries, see their tears, accept their repentance and deliver them.

The 42 months of Daniel's 70th week, when expended, will bring Antichrist's insane reign to an abrupt, dramatic conclusion. Jesus Christ, the King of kings and Lord of lords, shall return with those who have earlier met Him in the Rapture. And with the brightness of His glory and in righteousness He will judge and make war, followed by the armies in heaven, facing Antichrist's defiant armies at the last Battle of Armageddon. (Revelation 19:11-21.) The victory shall be complete — the total triumph over Antichrist, the False Prophet, and the kings of the earth and their armies which gathered together to make war against Christ.

And because they shall accept Jesus Christ as their Savior and Messiah, the Jews will be intimately identified with Christ in the millennium. The reins of world government will be in the benevolent control of the Messiah who will rule the earth in peace and righteousness from Jerusalem, the world capital. With the removal of the treacherous trinity by Christ enthroned, righteousness shall fill the earth as the waters cover the sea.

8

Occupy until Christ returns

THERE ARE EVENTS in a person's life that shake him to the core of his being; they make impressions and impacts upon his soul that cannot be erased. As long as my memory shall last, I shall carry with me upon the screen of my mind the graphic sign depicted by the Holy Spirit as I sat in a hotel room late one evening. I was preparing a message and had been reading my Bible, when suddenly I saw these words before me: It Is Later Than You Think.

One does not have visions of this nature often, else they would become commonplace. To me this was a rare experience and exceedingly precious. Again those words blazed before my eyes — It Is Later Than YOU Think. The word YOU stood out as if on fire.

It struck me with the force of a physical blow. Was I not aware? Was I not alert to what was going on in the realm of the spirit? Did I not discern God's timetable? I was shaken by that experience and have shared it with many thousands of people. Our days are numbered. Not only are our days numbered personally, but time limits for the human race have been established and He alone knows what those limits are. "But of that day and hour knoweth no man, no, not the angels in heaven, but my Father only" (Matthew 24:36).

Jesus said, "Be ye also ready: for in such an hour as ye think not the Son of man cometh" (Matthew 24:44).

This call for alertness does not suggest that we sell all that we possess and climb some hillside to await His coming, for Jesus also said, "Occupy till I come" (Luke 19:13). We do not discontinue erecting churches and building God's kingdom because we believe He is coming. A young minister asked me if he should continue and complete his education in view of the imminent return of the Lord. I answered, "I'd rather be trying to finish my education, in preparation to preach, even if He is coming tomorrow."

"What about my witness?" he asked.

"Witness while you're in school," I replied. "A pulpit is not the only place to win souls. Whatever you do for God, do it with all your might and 'occupy' till Jesus comes."

Deep down in your heart you must learn how to respond to Christ, how to conduct your daily affairs with an attitude pleasing to God, whether you are a preacher or a layman. Being "not of the world" does not refer merely to a physical posture. It concerns your spirit, your mind, and your heart. You can sit down to dinner with people who drink and not desire to drink. Jesus did that. He ate with publicans and sinners; He did not isolate himself from the stream of humanity. A Christian does not withdraw himself from society, he becomes a part of it in order to win men.

"Occupy till I come." In response to the Lord's command to reach the unreached, I have attempted for almost a quarter of a century to obey Him in a pragmatic and punctual manner. In 1947, He said to go to the people in large evangelical crusades and we did. The huge tent was stretched in nearly every major city across the United States and Canada. Millions of people were won to the Lord through the preaching of the good news of Jesus Christ. God said to lay hands on the people and pray for their healing and thousands of sick, diseased, disturbed, and dying persons have received the laying on of hands as we prayed the prayer of faith for God to raise them up and heal them. He told us to go into all nations and we have gone to almost 60 nations of the world. He said to build a university to multiply this ministry, and in 1963, starting with the same ingredient which God used when He created this earth — nothing — Oral Roberts University came into existence. Through God's leadership and guidance there is a campus with close to a thousand students, an outstanding faculty, and the finest of facilities. He said to raise up our students to go with us to take His healing power to the remotest bounds of the earth, where His light is dim, His voice is heard small and His healing power is not known. I was to work with the students and train them to hear His voice, and increasing numbers of faithful youth have stood with us as we confronted the people in their desperation and suffering. He said to train World Action Teams from the University to go into all the world and we are, nation by nation.

God told us to utilize all this experience, use all the talent on our team and campus to make an impact on this nation through the means of television. In 1954, when we first obeyed God to go on television, key men in the industry said it could not be done, that we could not film in the big tent, that we could not secure stations to run our program. But by God's grace we did. And for the first time, multitudes saw the results of God's healing power right in their own living rooms. In the spring of 1967, after 13 years of nationwide television, the Lord let me see that phase of our television ministry temporarily terminated so that I could devote my time and attention to our World Action program. In 1969, God gave us new marching orders to return to television with ORU and our World Action Teams in a program format that is reaching a potential audience 10 times the number attending churches, reaching all levels and ages. "Occupy till I come."

We have been entrusted with the opportunity to be Christians and soul winners at a time unparalleled in history. This is no time to be fearful and disobedient. There is no power on earth that can stop you or hinder you as you move forward in the center of God's will. I am convinced that the Lord is determined to reach this generation through dedicated, daring lives.

You may never go overseas, but you can be spreading the Good News where you are. The field is the world and your neighborhood is part of that world. You cannot afford to be idle. "Occupy till He comes."

Christ touches people, for Christ is where the lost are. Christ is where the bitter people are, where the violent are. He is also observing Christians who are not involved. They attend church but ignore the needs of people, whether unsaved, sick, or underprivileged. But I believe that Jesus Christ is urging us to touch somebody. You can touch people in numerous ways — with your hands, with your words, with your heart, with a smile, with a look, with your compassion and willingness to identify with their need. World Action is every Christian becoming a missionary Christian, a witness of Jesus where you are. Let us occupy until He comes! Maranatha!